Before and After
the Border

Before and After the Border

One Man's Journey Home

Ricardo O. Sánchez, PhD

Published by Journey Within, LLC
120 3rd St. #1694, Front Royal, VA 22630
https://www.eaglecondorcenter.org/

Library of Congress Control Number: 2024923680

ISBN 979-8-9919171-0-0 (Paperback)
ISBN 979-8-9919171-1-7 (eBook)

Keywords: Immigration, immigrant journey, American Dream, immigrant integration, human rights, immigration reform, border security, comprehensive immigration

Book cover illustration by Ricardo O. Sánchez
Book edited by Katherine Sánchez
Partial cover image of the U.S. flag © Adobe Stock. Used under license.

For permissions or inquiries, contact: editor@journeywithin.llc

DEDICATIONS

To all the immigrants in the Americas.
To their resilient spirit.

"Coming home is about coming back to the self, finding in the self a place of refuge, joy, and sanctuary."

~ bell hooks (Belonging: A Culture of Place)

FOREWORD

The best people to talk about the immigrant journey are immigrants themselves. I have conceptualized and written about the stages of migration from accountings shared with me, but Ricardo's narrative is compelling, heartbreaking, and truth-telling. Consistent in this book are his faith, persistence, sense of hope, and descriptions of the back-breaking, low-paying employment immigrants often take on to fulfill commitments back home and benefit this country. There is no time to slouch, and even if others take advantage of your naivete and fear, you know your purpose—to take care of those you left behind and to make a place in this country for yourself.

Ricardo's accounting of "before the border," tells us about the lengths he went in preparing to come the documented way, and then, the way far too many migrants have had to travel, with danger, hope, and no guarantee of getting to the other side. The migration journey is so well detailed that I felt I was going along with Ricardo, and his writing certainly raised my trepidations about what he and others would experience. Rosita and her son, fellow travelers, were a constant in his recollections. His upbringing taught him about caretaking and being concerned about other's well-being. Thus, it is not surprising that he has now a doctorate in Counseling and that he and his wife now lead a healing center.

Throughout his narrative, Ricardo also reveals his mistrust "before and after the border." But he did have "angels," individuals who became mentors, gifting him with hope and resolve to not give up, despite looming deportation challenges. These critical incidents or encounters had a profound impact on his thinking in the midst of emotional dissonance. With John, his older friend, he learned that he was not alone and that others who were U.S. born and employed also had disappointments they accepted and resolved. His friend John opened doors to Ricardo's educational goals, and Chief Raincrow Neale at American University gave him the break he needed in the formal structures. In Chief Raincrow Neale, he also found a spiritual connection to his Peruvian roots and his Inkan heritage. This was an important developmental time for Ricardo as he became more publicly outspoken, establishing *Amigos America* with John, developing connections with others, and giving others a space for belonging. In my experience, the immigrants I have known are optimistic and futuristic thinkers, which drives their motivation to cross the border. In their new destination, they demonstrate empathy and support others, as Ricardo did with Rosita and her son. Even after he was in D.C., he wondered about them and how they might be doing.

Ricardo endeavored to find legal ways to stay in the country that became his new home and a land to dream and hope. Meeting Kathy was a pivotal part of his confidence-building, sense of self-efficacy, and hope for a future in the strange country that rejected him so often. She was a "major" angel, and their friendship led to a commitment to marriage. However, as with all life in the post-migration phase, learning how to negotiate new norms, accept help, and believe that others believe in you did not come easy. Questioning his self-worth was another part of the emotional struggle Ricardo experienced. Those who work in counseling or other settings with immigrants and refugees know that trust is a paramount hurdle.

Just when you think you are "home free," immigrants continue to get surprised. Ricardo recounts his journey back to his homeland, to Lima and Arequipa, where he grew up. Did Kathy marry him so he could get his papers? With a white woman like Kathy, would he forget his roots? Ricardo had to prove his authenticity to his long-term friends and even family members. Though he did not say it directly, immigrants who have "made it" by becoming documented, may experience resentment and distancing from friends and family. It is a double-edged sword, at times, to achieve your dreams.

The immigrant journey, which I have captured in my scholarship as having pre-migration, migration-specific, and post-migration eras, is rarely known by non-immigrants or individuals whose families have not recently experienced the migration process. The focus continues to be on black and brown migrants, not those who continue to arrive from European countries. Although it is a fact that the majority of persons in the U.S. are descendants of immigrants from England, Ireland, Italy, Japan, Greece, Russia, China, Korea, the Philippines, and the rest of the world, individuals deny their roots or simply move into a xenophobic mindset. It is a challenge for Latinx immigrants like Ricardo to be invisible as they go about making economic contributions to the U.S. On the political stage, they are demonized ruthlessly by racist politicians. Those who are not immigrants, need to pause and learn about how they are beneficiaries of immigrant labor, optimism, and good-will.

Ricardo is clear about what grounds him, and these beliefs deepened in the relationship with a soulmate—Kathy. Faith, spirituality, finding the best in others, and continuing his life's journey grounded in his belief in humanity are his lived experiences. My hope is that, by reading this book, readers will become more curious about their own family history and perhaps develop empathy for immigrants, who make a difference in everyone's lives. One's identity as an immigrant never fades but given more balanced visibility through books such as this one, perhaps others can come to appreciate and respect the immigrant path.

Patricia Arredondo, EdD
President, Arredondo Advisory Group
Faculty Fellow, Fielding Graduate University

ACKNOWLEDGMENTS

It is difficult to write and publish a book from the shadows. I lost count of how many times over the years that I grabbed a pen and paper and started to write, only to stop again. In the mid-1990s, I bought a pack of cassette tapes and started recording key moments of the journey. But even then, it felt like the story was just beginning. Maybe it just needed to play out for a while and wait for the right time.

The truth is that the story of a first-generation migrant doesn't really have an end. The collection of experiences that occur along the journey, each worthy of being shared, continues to grow but is never complete. And yet, after almost four decades of living in the United States, it feels as if the immigrant within and without has come full cycle.

When Covid-19 arrived, it was like a signal for me: It is time. The pandemic provided time for introspection so I could organize all the experiences side by side, integrate them, and make sense of it all. The alien and the citizen, the vigilante and the settler, the student and the teacher, the wounded soul and the healer, the unaccompanied minor and the self-supporting adult, the *before and after*.

As a young immigrant, I needed a place to land, people who I could relate to, and a community that would accept me for who I am. I acknowledge and appreciate every encounter I have had with my South, Central, and North American relatives and with people from around the world. I treasure every day I have spent in this ancient land, Turtle

Island, the United States of America. It truly is the land of the brave, the land of innovators, the land of immigrants, the land of opportunities, the land where dreams come true. I am grateful for all my relations and all my encounters with them.

TABLE OF CONTENTS

AUTHOR'S NOTE

While this book is based on real events and people, some names and identifying details have been changed to protect the privacy of those involved. The historical events and personal stories within are true to the best of my knowledge, but they are also filtered through my perspective as an author. I have aimed to capture the essence of the immigrant experience, but any errors or omissions are my own. I hope my story inspires people to understand and appreciate the true experiences, challenges, and resilience of immigrants in the United States.

PROLOGUE

"The journey of a thousand miles begins with a single step"

~ Lao Tzu

In a way, this book is the story of almost all of us. It pays respect to the first-generation members of your own family, whether they migrated seven or two generations ago from China, Germany, India, Mexico, Nigeria, or some other country. It is a call to cherish our relations and our lost connections and to honor modern-day immigrants as well as our ancestors, especially those who migrated to this land. I hope reading my story will help you imagine what it must have been like for them as immigrants who were seeing North America for the first time. Perhaps then, you will realize how much we have in common and that we are connected through a transgenerational journey to this united nation that must now build its future on the backbone of our common roots.

The story is both personal and collective—it will take you on a trip into a world of the *first-generation* immigrant community, a community of over 11 million undocumented and 45 million documented migrants in the U.S. As you follow along on this journey, you will get a closer look at the day-to-day experiences of undocumented youth in America—

the multiple ways we settle, adjust, adapt, or relocate within America to find a place we can call home. You will visit the places I have visited and experience my emotions as I struggled to adapt to a different sociocultural reality.

As you read, you will see how my arrival in the United States was highly influenced by sociopolitical and economic events—the U.S. economic expansion at the turn of the 20th century, the decades-long Cold War, and the subsequent proxy wars in Central America—all playing out right next door. Negligence, government corruption, corporate power and greed, and unequal trade deals were part of the mix that fed the past and current waves of internal and international migration that occurred when people just could not take their local realities anymore. My hope is that through these pages, the unspoken brotherhood and sisterhood of this marginalized population will have a voice and will begin to be understood by mainstream North Americans. In our collective search for unity and healing, understanding the "immigrant *and* emigrant" side of the story is essential to address the challenges associated with immigration in our country.

Lastly, I hope you will see that migration is a natural phenomenon that has been undertaken by birds, insects, and animals, including humans, for millennia. Although human migration is complicated by ideologies, policies, and documentation status, for many, it is an important element of individual and family development. Migration is about caring for the well-being of children, adolescents, adults, and parents who relocate to look for a better future, work, better themselves, and contribute positively to society. It is what people do in order to evolve, grow, progress, look for safety, and ultimately, find self-realization.

CHAPTER 1

The Immigrant Within

"Once I thought to write a history of the immigrants in America. Then I discovered that the immigrants were American history."

~ Oscar Handlin

"Flight attendants prepare for landing." Words that I couldn't understand, but I knew exactly what they meant. We're landing soon! And you must act as if you have done this many times. Pretend you are a frequent flyer and you know the off-boarding rituals and all the hallways of this airport by heart.

As the plane gradually dropped in elevation, my heart rate accelerated, developing a sort of a chaotic dance made up of wishful thinking and terrifying scenarios. *Surely, Aunt Juana would be waiting there for me with open arms. Or maybe she sent someone to pick me up who will be holding up a cardboard sign with my name on it… or, oh my God, immigration officers will be waiting for me! Two men in black with emotionless faces will block my way, handcuff me, and put me back on the plane!*

It was impossible to stop all the crazy scenarios playing out in my head. I felt anxious, confused, excited, and euphoric, but also, ashamed, foreign, vulnerable, and disoriented. How was I going to keep the sea of emotions invisible, so people wouldn't see them all over my face? With great effort, I forced all my emotions deep down. My body was sweating, but at least my face looked relaxed. I quietly wiped the palms of my hands on my pants to dry them, but the sweat kept wetting my hands.

Throughout the overnight flight from Los Angeles to Washington, D.C. in January 1987, I had been wide awake and hyperalert, but I'd kept my eyes closed, pretending to be asleep. I'd pretended because I did not want to talk to anyone. A conversation in English would have been a disaster, and I wanted to avoid conversations with curious, bilingual gringos.[1] What if they were informants or undercover immigration officers? I didn't want to take any chances, so I had pretended to be asleep.

As the plane approached its destination, I opened my eyes for a couple of seconds to look down at my running shoes to make sure they were presentable. I noticed the mud had dried, but they were still covered with dust. I slowly bent my knees to tuck my feet underneath the seat so that no one would see them. I was running on fear. It was needed. It kept me going and was my only companion.

---

[1] A colloquial term primarily used in Latin American countries to refer to foreigners, especially those from English-speaking countries like the United States. The term often refers to white, non-Hispanic people.

I don't know if he was talking about an immigrant's journey, but poet Kahlil Gibran[2] once wrote, "before entering the sea, a river trembles with fear. She looks back at the path she has traveled, from the peaks of the mountains, the long winding road crossing forests and villages… but there is no way to go back… The river needs to take the risk of entering the ocean because only then will fear disappear." All I knew was that *I* was about enter a sea of unknowns, trembling with fear. My one-way flight was about to land, and there was no turning back. It was a dramatic rite of passage to adulthood via the unknown.

As the plane continued to descend, flashbacks of my arrival at the Tijuana bus terminal at the beginning to my journey to the United States were still fresh in my mind, making my heart beat like a drum against my chest. The Mexican Federales had left a permanent scar on my soul. Group humiliation, mistreatment, and assault can take all involved to a very dark place. At 18, I never thought I would witness so much pain or experience such extreme fear and desperation. I've dreaded bus terminals and airplane landings since then, but at least this time I was alone. If I were detained, no one would notice. Realizing I wasn't doing myself any favors by rehashing recent memories, I tucked the thoughts away. *I'll think about that later*, I told myself.

The landing was smooth, thankfully. I thanked the Creator for the safe landing and asked for protection with every

---

[2] Kahlil Gibran (1883–1931), a Lebanese-American poet, writer, visual artist, and philosopher, was best known for *The Prophet*, a collection of poetic essays on love, life, and spirituality. Blending Eastern and Western philosophies, his work inspiring readers worldwide with its timeless wisdom and lyrical style.

step I took. "*Please protect me. Make me invisible when I pass through the airport hallways,*" I silently begged the loving, bearded white Father in the skies.

As I walked away from the airplane and into the walkways of Washington National Airport—later renamed for the president at the time, Ronald Reagan—I felt my anxiety begin to lessen. Everyone was walking fast and minding their own business, to my great relief. I, too, started to walk fast as my eyes scanned the area, searching for Aunt Juana. Before I knew it, my fast-paced walk had led me to the main doorway that faced the parking lot. *Where is she? Did I miss her?*

I turned around and went back inside the airport. *Perhaps she is looking for me in another walkway*, I thought. I had been disconnected from the world for weeks during my journey across the Mexican border, and I realized there was no way she could have known the exact date and time of my arrival.

I walked all the walkways but did not see anyone I knew. Each time I passed someone wearing a uniform, whether they were airport security or simply a mean-looking janitor, I grew more anxious, even as I tried to act nonchalant. I knew I had to avoid making naïve mistakes at all costs to avoid raising eyebrows. Although I wanted to make a phone call, I didn't know how payphones worked in North America, so I decided not to try, afraid I would look blatantly foreign and dumb. Instead, I sat down to wait for Aunt Juana. Refusing to believe that she wouldn't come, I waited from 9 am to 4 pm, but no one showed up. Hungry and mentally exhausted, I decided to wait outside in the parking lot because I was increasingly afraid that security personnel would notice me and get suspicious.

Out on the sidewalk, many taxicabs were lined up, and the drivers were asking people coming out of the airport if they needed a ride. I stood there for a few seconds, watching the driver-passenger dynamic to learn how to ask for a ride.

Whooooosssshhhh!! A massive, long metal capsule that looked like something from Star Trek flew by above my head on a raised platform. As I continued to stare at this UFO,[3] I realized it was a modern electric train, so advanced and quiet that it took my breath away. It was my first encounter with the metro subway system, and I was stunned. Then, it hit me: *I was in the United States of America, the most technologically advanced country in the world!*

As I processed this epiphany, it dawned on me that all this staring upwards with my jaw on the floor was probably making me look like a real alien. So, I quickly regrouped and began to pay attention to the African taxi driver who was talking to me from across his car. My ears heard: "Blah, blah, blah, something, something, blah, blah, blah, amigo?" He asked a few more questions that I didn't understand, but through my previous observations, I deduced that he wanted me to jump into his taxicab. I looked at him and shrugged, trying to guess what he was saying and trying to appear agreeable. Although I couldn't answer his questions, the driver realized that yes, I needed his services.

I didn't have an address to give him. Instead, I handed him a slip of paper with Aunt Juana's phone number and pretended to hold a phone to my ear, splaying out my thumb and pinky finger to represent the ear and mouth pieces. He

---

[3] A UFO (Unidentified Flying Object) refers to any aerial object or phenomenon that cannot be immediately identified or explained. Often associated with potential extraterrestrial activity, but not always.

took the paper and we walked over to the payphone outside the door to the airport. Having arrived with zero money in my pocket, I could not even give him a dime for the phone call. So, he pulled a coin out of his own pocket and dialed the number I had given him. Luckily for me, someone was home, and that person gave him my Aunt's address. A few seconds later, the driver hung up and said something that I guessed probably meant, "Let's go!"

The moment I sat down in the back seat of the taxi with my "luggage," a plastic grocery bag containing exactly one pair of pants and one pair of shoes, I felt immense relief. As we drove along the Washington Parkway toward Wisconsin Avenue, it was hard to keep my jaw off the floor. The beautiful scenery and wide, curvy highways filled with so many modern cars amazed me, not to mention all the traffic signs, brick homes, and buildings. For 20 minutes, I completely zoned out and let my eyes take in this unplanned tour of the West side of the nation's capital, complete with a magnificent sunset over the Potomac River. The driver said something and stretched his right hand toward the passenger window, I looked in the direction he was pointing and saw the Washington Monument, its obelisk visible from a mile away. I knew what it was because of the countless American movies I had watched growing up. It was a heavenly ride in my new America,[4] though it lasted only a few minutes.

---

[4] In this book, I use the term "America" interchangeably with "the United States," as is common in colloquial and academic discourse, However, it is important to point out that "America" technically refers to the entire landmass comprising both North and South America as well as Central America and the Caribbean. The Americas are home to a diverse range of nations, cultures, and peoples, including those from Latin

The driver parked across from the National Cathedral on Wisconsin Avenue. I looked out the window and noticed the gardens, with bushes carved into attractive shapes like hearts and bears, on the right side of cathedral. *That's probably where my aunt's mansion is.*

As the driver parked the car, I felt a huge sense of relief at the thought of living in the comfort of a mansion in the nation's capital. *My journey of 4,000 miles has finally ended, and soon I will have a comfortable space to sleep and plan my future.*

The driver, with his thick African accent, said, "We've arrived, amigo." As I looked across the street at the National Cathedral and "my" mansion right next to it, a stranger opened the door from the sidewalk side. *Hola, amigo, ya llegaste! Puedes bajarte.* "Hello, my friend, you made it! You can get out."

He paid for the ride, tipped the driver, and closed the door behind me. "My name is Sergio, welcome!" he said in Spanish. "Glad to meet you, Sergio, I'm Ricardo," I said. "Your aunt told me you would be arriving sometime this week, but she didn't know the exact date. I guess she was expecting you to call," Sergio said. "Follow me, this way," he added.

As he walked, leading me away from the mansion toward some apartment buildings in the opposite direction, my skepticism returned. *What if this guy was a robber? Or an undercover immigration agent? Why were we walking toward a run-down apartment building instead of crossing the street to the mansion?*

America, whose experiences and contributions are central to discussions on immigration.

"How was the trip? How long did it take you? How many people came with you? Did they catch you?" Sergio seemed to want to know everything at once. My initial friendliness quickly vanished as he bombarded me with questions. *Who is this complete stranger?!* I really wasn't ready to tell him anything. After all I had gone through, I didn't even trust my own shadow. But as we walked, something told me Sergio was legit. He was just curious, like any other immigrant would be who probably had gone through a similar journey.

I answered a few questions without going into detail. With a serious face, I then asked, "Doesn't my Aunt Juana live in that mansion over there? Why are we walking in the opposite direction?" Sergio burst out laughing, as if I had told the world's biggest joke. His laughter stung. I felt annoyed, embarrassed, and hurt, and my mind reeled as all my dreams of living a privileged life evaporated and reality sunk in. *Why would Aunt Juana tell my family that she lived in a mansion all these years? Why would she lie to us?*

With everything that had happened, the last thing I needed was more confusion about the place where I was going to stay. But I was not in a position to complain. I had not slept, bathed, or eaten well in days, and I was exhausted, in shock, paranoid, broke, and feeling completely out of place. So, I forced myself to calm down and focus on my present situation as we walked toward the apartment building. "Thank you, Sergio, I will pay you back for the taxi ride as soon as I find some work," I said. He said, "No worries, man, I know how hard it is in the beginning."

We entered the small apartment, and there was Aunt Juana, wearing her black banquet server uniform with a white long-sleeve shirt, a black bowtie, and her usual plump-cheeked smile. She had just arrived home from work and greeted me warmly, much to my relief, as she was the only blood relative I had in this strange country.

I had only met Aunt Juana a few times before during my childhood on her occasional visits to Peru. She asked me the same questions that Sergio had asked earlier on the sidewalk, and I felt more at ease talking about my journey with her. She was not too surprised by my stories, as some of the tenants in her apartment had had similar journeys.

"Did you call your parents?" she asked. "Not yet," I said, "but I would like to call today, if possible." She said, "Yes, just let them know you arrived safely. They must be anxious to hear from you. But keep it short, please, because long distance calls are extremely expensive." "Thanks, Aunt Juana, I will keep it short," I assured her.

I called my parents for the first time since I had left my hometown almost a month before. I figured that they had worried about me enough during the many days of my journey, so I decided not to tell them about my traumatic experiences. Instead, I focused on how beautiful the ride was from the airport, the futuristic train, and everything that had amazed me. I told them I would write letters to keep the telephone costs down. In 1987, AT&T had a monopoly on long-distance telephone service, and a 30-minute call to South America cost about $38. Later, I would learn that every immigrant had horror stories about how much of their hard-earned money they had to spend just to pay the phone bill.

That evening, I met Sergio's roommate Fernando, a Peruvian from the Amazon region. "You can share the room over there with Sergio and Fernando," my Aunt Juana said, pointing across the apartment hallway. Through humor, the three of us connected quickly. We had all left our real families back home, and now, we were living under the same roof. We also shared the immigrant-experience connection, including an omnipresent fear of the unknown and an understanding of the struggles associated with undocumented life in the U.S., and we instinctively knew we had to watch each other's backs. I was four years younger than them, and soon, they became like my brothers. Fernando told me I reminded him of his younger sibling, while he reminded me of my older brother.

Aunt Juana herself was a single mother with three adopted children, and they lived with us in the apartment. A young family of four also lived in the room next door in the same apartment. Although crowded by American standards, sharing tight space was nothing new for us Peruvians. It just wasn't what I had expected because during her occasional visits to Peru in the past, when my siblings and I had asked Aunt Juana about her home, she had told us that she lived in a mansion. That's how I had gotten the impression of her as my rich aunt in the United States.

It turns out that Aunt Juana hadn't lied, though. She had migrated to the U.S. during the Nixon administration in the early 1970s, a few years after finishing high school in Peru. A rich family of diplomats who lived in Potomac, Maryland brought her over from Peru to be their live-in nanny. Working at the family's mansion was exhausting. Although she was supposed to work 40 hours per week, like most immigrant nannies, she ended up working 6 days a week from dawn until everyone went to sleep. She was expected to wake up at 5:00 a.m. to prepare breakfast for the family and get the children ready for school. Then, she had to clean the large house, cook the meals, and take care of the children after school and on weekends; plus, she had to be "on call" at night when the children couldn't sleep or were sick. She was loved by the family's children, and they called her "mom" and expected her to tell them stories and give them daily good night kisses. She loved the children as much as they loved her, though, so she never complained.

A "bonus" of working at the mansion was that she was asked to work part-time as a banquet server whenever the family held a reception for their friends or other diplomats. In those situations, she at least enjoyed having the chance to socialize with other hired servers, cooks, and guests.

Like many nannies, Aunt Juana was overworked. But unlike most undocumented nannies, at least she was able to travel overseas on family trips and enjoy a month of paid vacation, which she used to visit friends and family in Peru. Generous to the core, she always brought presents and souvenirs for her friends and relatives on her occasional visits home. However, very few knew how much she had to sacrifice to save money throughout the year to buy all those presents.

Aunt Juana lived with the diplomat family for over a decade, staying almost until the family's children went off to college. That was when she was finally able to move on with her own search for the American Dream, becoming a U.S. citizen in the mid-1980s. But leaving the family meant moving out of the mansion, too. After she left, she landed a job as a banquet waitress in Washington, D.C. and moved to the working-class neighborhood apartment she now generously shared with me and many others. Although she dreamed of enjoying a life with a partner and becoming the mother of an adopted child, she had no luck with romantic relationships. However, the most important part of her dream came true when three orphaned siblings from her hometown were given up for adoption. She gladly accepted them into her life and raised them with love and kindness. Learning Aunt Juana's story was eye-opening because I had no idea how many sacrifices she had to make, how hard she had to work, and how long it takes to achieve some semblance of the American Dream.

We Didn't Cross the Border, the Border Crossed Us

Coming to the United States has educated me in ways that college never could have matched. It has taught me how far back the origins of the "American Dream" extend and why so many immigrants risk their entire families' lives, walking thousands of miles and crossing rivers and deserts to reach the United States. As I made my journey to the U.S., I met migrants fleeing situations in Central America that were similar to or even worse than mine, often life threatening. I was part of a wave of millions of new immigrants that had started a decade or so before I arrived in 1987. This influx created an irresistible opportunity for politicians, and many took full advantage, blaming us for all of society's woes, from crime to economic trouble. Not surprisingly, turning immigrants into scapegoats has only fed negative public perceptions around immigration.

The truth was—and is—that immigration is not the problem; it is only the symptom. How do I know this? A quick look at history tells the real story. It goes back to the initial commercial interactions between the U.S. and Central and South America after the American Civil War and the second industrial revolution (1870-1914). During that era of exploration and economic growth in the U.S., a wave of innovations birthed new corporations that served as the engines behind economic progress. A few of the most powerful players in each industry went after riches far South of the border. However, they didn't realize the impact this would have on migration patterns for the next hundred years.

John Rockefeller's Standard Oil Company, for example, significantly shaped global business practices with its strategy of monopolizing the oil industry. Utilizing tactics like vertical integration—fierce prevention or elimination of competitors—it set precedents for efficiency and division of labor. Rockefeller's vast wealth from Standard Oil afforded him influence in oil-rich regions, impacting U.S. foreign policy and occasionally inciting armed conflicts abroad. Although it was dissolved in 1911 due to antitrust violations, Standard Oil's aggressive tactics persisted, influencing other corporations globally for decades to come.

Natural resource extraction and fruit production companies in Central America mirrored this approach of using financial power to influence public policy. They formed alliances with local Central American oligarchs to control channels of extraction and acquire cheap agricultural goods, creating so-called "Banana Republics."[5] These alliances fueled

---

[5] The term "Banana Republic" originated in the early 20th century and was popularized by American writer O. Henry in his 1904 book, *Cabbages and Kings*. It refers to politically unstable and economically dependent Central American countries, whose governments were often

America's growing economy and provided plenty of financial perks for U.S. corporations at the expense of Central America's peasant-class workers. As expansionist systems grew, the Banana Republic model wasn't confined to Central America; it laid the foundation that extended into South America and elsewhere.

The economic changes arising from the entry of international corporations into Latin America spurred internal migrations within many Latin American nations, drawing people to industries backed by U.S. expansion. But lax regulations kept the workers poor, and working conditions saw little improvement. In the late 1940s and 1950s, U.S. political and military interventions worsened the economic gaps and caused environmental harm, fostering discontent and impeding progress in Central and South America. This led to proxy wars during the Cold War years (1947-1989), as the growing instability in Central America fueled violence and human rights abuses, prompting many to seek refuge in the United States.

As all this was happening, U.S. radio, television programs, and movies saturated the airwaves in Latin America. More than 160 million Latin American consumers were hooked on U.S. dramas, comedies, and Westerns, which fed them a steady diet of American/Eurocentric values and exceptionalism. U.S.-made toys and big-ticket items such as cars, trucks, and airplanes were in high demand among Latin

---

manipulated by foreign corporations, particularly the United Fruit Company (now called Chiquita Brands International). These companies controlled large portions of the economy by monopolizing banana production and exports, which led to the exploitation of local labor, corruption, and the establishment of puppet governments that prioritized corporate interests over citizen well-being.

American consumers, including in Peru. Many U.S. manufacturers held monopoly status, easily eliminating the local Peruvian competition. Major players such as Coca Cola, Marlboro, Proctor & Gamble, Johnson & Johnson, Exxon Mobil, and leading car manufacturers capitalized on the opportunity, enjoying oligopoly or monopoly access to Peru and other Latin American markets for decades. Corporations set up satellite offices in capital cities like Lima, which accelerated internal migration from rural areas to the capital. The concentration of wealth in a handful of districts in Lima and a few other cities didn't escape government notice. Urban hubs received most of the attention and services, leaving rural and indigenous communities underserved. Internal migration to the cities intensified and by the mid-1950s, Lima and other urban centers in Peru struggled to keep pace with the demographic explosion, resulting in gaps in basic services such as water and electricity, and insufficient roads, schools, medical clinics, and other infrastructure. This contributed to increased poverty, malnutrition, and crime, fueling social discontent and domestic political-ideological conflicts.

Watching American shows gave people a taste of the American lifestyle and consequently, showed them what they were missing out on. Whether they knew it or not, Hollywood executives were Americanizing Latin America by entertaining its people. In Peru, the American Dream became synonymous with experiencing the lifestyle portrayed by Hollywood. Only the wealthiest families in Lima could afford American lifestyles akin to those in Miami or Beverly Hills. For the rest of the Peruvian population, the American Dream became a lifelong pursuit. Youth in Westernized

Peruvian metropolises adopted a neo-colonial mentality, viewing anything from North America or Europe as superior to local ingenuity and culture.

I guess most of us know that consuming a steady diet of fantasies has real-life consequences, but I wonder how many people realize just how powerful those fantasies can be. That they can entice millions of people into moving from rural communities to urban ones, for example? Or from their home countries to a new nation? Peru was hardly an island in this context. Each nation in Latin America had its own unique economic and socio-political transformation; but all were shaped by the United States' prominent transnational influence. While mainstream America is rightfully concerned about mass migration, I hopeful that raising awareness about the root causes and historical context of mass migration will soften the sometimes harsh political rhetoric around it and improve understanding of immigrants among mainstream Americans.

American Before Migration

In 1945, when he was 5 years old, my father, Samuel, migrated with his family from a Quechua-speaking village in the Valley of Volcanoes to Arequipa, a Westernized city in Southern Peru. His father had just died, and without his support, the family needed to move to an economically modernized city to find jobs. My dad's real journey into adulthood commenced at age 12, when his mother also died. Along with his four siblings, he worked in multiple jobs as a *chuli*—a typically indigenous, underpaid teenage jack-of-all-trades—just to survive. At first, he made just enough money to get by, but as he got older and gained a reputation as a hard worker, he was able to find slightly better-paying gigs.

Navigating the tumultuous terrain of his teenage years, my father began to embrace the rebellious and adventurous spirit of the 1950's American radio and film industry, which had spread throughout the Western hemisphere. The influence of iconic films like *Rebel Without a Cause*, *Ben-Hur*, and *Doctor Zhivago* resonated deeply with Peruvian adolescents. As soon as he could afford it, Samuel joined his friends by wearing black leather jackets and blue jeans, channeling the styles of James Dean and Elvis. They did their best to sing English songs by Paul Anka, Chubby Checker, and Buddy Holly.

Upon reaching the age of 18 in 1958, my father embraced a new chapter as an apprentice mechanic for a local bus line in Arequipa. Surrounded by friends in the urban transportation industry, he spent his weekends with his group of pals, who celebrated their hard work during the week at lively gatherings filled with Peruvian and American music. They had a unique camaraderie, bound by their shared desire to pursue the American Dream in Arequipa. With Marlboro cigarettes dangling from their lips and shots of Pisco[6] mixed with Coca Cola in hand, the rock & roll music they loved bridged all language gaps, whether the lyrics were in English, Spanish, or Quechua.[7]

---

[6] Pisco is an alcoholic variety of grape aguardiente, produced in Peru since the late 16th century.

[7] Quechua is the most widely used indigenous language in the Americas, spoken by approximately 14 million people, mostly in Peru, Bolivia, Ecuador, Chile, Argentina, and Colombia. Originally called Runasimi (the people's language), it was the official language of Tawantinsuyu (the Inka nation) prior to the Spanish colonization.

Unbeknownst to my father, his magnetic presence didn't go unnoticed. Across from the dusty bus mechanic shop, my mother, Betty, couldn't help but be captivated by this handsome mechanic in his black boots and greasy blue jeans. After watching him for months, their paths finally intertwined by chance one day when my father, sporting his James Dean leather jacket, met Betty, a Sophia Loren look-alike, during his other job as a bus fare collector. Who was that beautiful young woman sitting in the front row of seats on his bus? Samuel stood up straighter, turned on his James Dean swagger, and took a few short steps to stand next to the lovely lady who had captured his attention. Their short conversation ended with him asking her out to the movies that weekend. After that first date, he found out where she lived, and a few days later, showed up under her window to serenade her with the most romantic Elvis tunes he knew, which, fortunately for him, had been translated into Spanish! Within a few weeks, Samuels' life took a turn for the better as he and Betty became a couple.

Several years into his relationship with my mother, Samuel persuaded his best friend Mario to join the Peruvian Air Force with him. As an extension of his fascination with the American lifestyle, my father had developed a profound admiration for the U.S. military. Growing up immersed in war comics and films like *Doctor Zhivago, Storm Over the Pacific, Flying Tigers, and Casablanca,* he paradoxically equated individual freedom with the structured confines of a soldier's barracks.

Joining the Peruvian Air Force meant that Samuel and Mario had to move to Lima, the epicenter of dreams and innovation. As Peru's capital city, Lima housed not only the latest commercial and military airplanes but also the hottest fashions, movies, and inventions arriving from the United States. Convinced that Lima held his destiny, Samuel prepared to explore the world. Betty, understanding the significance of Samuel's aspiration, agreed to wait for him to complete his service before tying the knot.

In the scorching summer of 1962, Betty and Samuel bid each other farewell at Arequipa's bus terminal with promises to write daily and to reunite after basic training. In Lima, Samuel and Mario joined a racially diverse cohort of Peruvian youth, including whites, indigenous people, *mestizos*, and blacks. Stationed at the Air Force base, Samuel became part of the Peruvian Air Force Military Police Unit, maneuvering everything from police motorcades to military trucks. His fascination with American-made military equipment grew, and he eagerly participated in trainings, often provided by American instructors. He completed parachute training and made his inaugural jump from an airplane. Experiencing free fall from 30,000 feet, he realized he was precisely where he needed to be at that moment. A sense of invincibility overcame him as he literally touched the sky, living out his American Dream in Peru.

Back in Arequipa, Betty grappled with the fear of losing Samuel to the military life, terrified that he might never return. However, Samuel remained steadfast in his promise, sending letters that bridged the distance and sustained their connection.

From Peru to Vietnam?

One day, following a 5:00 a.m. parachute training session, an officer relayed a message from upper command to all servicemen:

> While Peru maintains neutrality in the war between our primary ally, the United States and Vietnam, the Peruvian Air Force is forming a platoon of volunteer parachute personnel to be ready in the event that our ally from the North requires additional support in their war effort. We need volunteers to join the South American allied forces as "standby" support for the U.S. in Vietnam. Those who accept this invitation may be asked to join the volunteer platoons being formed in Brazil and Argentina. If our North American ally needs our collaboration due to continuous war complications in Southeast Asia, the Peruvian Air Force will be ready to send a select group of our bravest airmen and parachutists to join their troops at an airbase in the U.S. From there, you would be deployed for an 18-month tour. All volunteers who are called to serve would receive double their salary and a special bonus upon their return. We understand that this is not an easy decision, and the risk of dying for our ally in a foreign land is real. Those of you who wish to consider this option have two weeks to decide.

Upon hearing the communique, my father immediately made his decision. Amidst the crowded ranks, he raised his hand and declared, "I'll go!" Mario turned to him in amazement, exclaiming, "Are you crazy?" But realizing Samuel's earnestness, Mario also raised his hand and yelled, "I will go, too!" A few others said they would seriously consider the offer, promising to provide their answers in two weeks. For my father and Mario, the prospect of fighting in Vietnam resonated deeply. It was a chance to push their dream of soldierhood to the limit. To them, it meant standing alongside the best airpower on earth to thwart the advance of communism, whatever that meant. In essence, for these two fearless young men, joining the Americans in the fight was the highest honor and the climax of their human expression.

For the rest of the day, Samuel was on cloud nine, daydreaming about flying in a C-130 Hercules plane, or "Herk," as they were known. Or maybe he would fly in a C-124 Globemaster II, the plane with "clamshell" doors, hydraulic ramps in the front, and elevators in the back! Those were the latest and most revolutionary planes of the time. Both were on the wish list of the Peruvian Air Force. That afternoon, Samuel sent a passionate letter home to Arequipa to let Betty know about his decision. Mario wrote a letter to his parents, who owned the bus service, sharing the news.

That night in Arequipa, located 600 miles south of Lima, Betty suddenly felt nauseous and weak, nearly fainting. It was as if her soul was intertwined with Samuel's, and she sensed something was wrong. To restore her strength, Betty's mother Elena prepared a cup of herbal tea. Betty drank the tea and went to bed early, but she couldn't shake the foreboding feeling that something had happened to Samuel. Unbeknownst to her, as she was laying down, Samuel had just picked up his pen and begun writing to her about his recent experiences with the FAP, the Peruvian Air Force.

My Dearest Betty,
I hope this letter finds you in good health and high spirits. I couldn't wait to share some incredible news that has come my way. An amazing opportunity has presented itself, and

it involves being a part of a "standby" platoon here at the air base that will be ready for deployment overseas to collaborate with the U.S., in case help is needed in the war against Vietnam. My dear friend Mario will be alongside me in this adventure. If the U.S. decides to call on our support, my assignment would take 18 months. Although the prospect of being away from you is daunting, I want you to know that I won't be alone in this.

The compensation they are offering is quite substantial, and they have promised a generous bonus upon our return. I can't help but imagine the life we will build together after this experience. Picture this—a beautiful home, perhaps even a Jeep parked in the driveway, and the joy of a big family with five kids, our own little basketball team! (Isn't that a delightful thought?).

I'll catch the bus to Arequipa this Friday and will eagerly count the minutes until I can see your beautiful face again on Saturday. Being with you before embarking on this journey means the world to me.

As I pledged to you a year ago, my love for you remains unwavering. You are the sole occupant of my thoughts, the beating of my heart. Distance cannot diminish the love and commitment I feel for you. Please hold onto that truth until we meet again.

With all my love and longing,
Samuel

Samuel sent the letter that night, and within a few days, it reached Arequipa. As was her routine, Betty visited the bus terminal on her way to work to check for letters or packages from Lima. Even before opening Samuel's letter, her stomach felt uneasy, as if she had caught a stomach virus. Upon opening the letter from the man who had been her first and only love, Betty couldn't believe the words before her. She somehow managed to walk to the phone service dispatcher, rent a phone booth, and place two calls. First, she informed her boss that she was unwell and wouldn't be at work that day. Next, she dialed the Chorrillos Air Force Base in Lima.

"This is a family emergency call for Private Sánchez from Arequipa," she announced, as only emergency calls were permitted at the base.

"Private Sánchez, you have an emergency call from Arequipa!" echoed the dispatcher through the intercom.

Upon hearing the announcement, Samuel hurried into the office, expressed his gratitude to the dispatcher, and entered the phone booth. Attempting to compose herself amid her disappointment and pain, Betty struggled to articulate her thoughts coherently. Despite her best efforts, a flood of emotions overwhelmed her.

"Why are you doing this?" she cried. "I've been counting the days until your return from the service in 10 months! Do you realize that thousands of people are dying every day in that war, a war that isn't even ours? Have you thought about their families, their loved ones? ...Me?" Her words poured out in an emotional jumble.

Caught off guard and aware that the phone booth lacked a door, making it impossible to have a private conversation, Samuel fought to maintain his composure. Speaking somewhat tersely, all he could manage was to say was, "I hope the surgery goes well. I will be praying for you, and I will see you on Saturday. Take care."

The 18-hour bus journey to Arequipa felt like 18 days. Instead of daydreaming about flying in the Herks, visiting the Air Force base in the U.S., or parachuting into strange lands in Southeast Asia, Samuel began to reflect, questioning his own judgment and the decision he had made. "Perhaps, I am being too selfish...What if they let Betty go with me to the U.S.? Maybe she can wait there for me while I go to Vietnam... What if I only go for 10 months?... What if..." The bus was arriving in Arequipa, and Samuel was running out of "what ifs." None of his scenarios included breaking up with Betty, though.

Following a simultaneously awkward and passionate greeting at the bus station, Betty and Samuel embarked on a lengthy walk that culminated in a park. Their Saturday was consumed by conversation, occasional arguments, tears, and reflections on the trajectory of their relationship. Betty finally drew a line in the sand, staunchly declaring that if Samuel joined the "standby" platoon to fight in Vietnam, their relationship was over. Recognizing the gravity of the situation and what was at stake, Samuel spent the next two days gaining perspective and soul-searching. Ultimately, he chose love over war, to Betty's immense relief. Upon learning that Samuel had decided not to join the "standby" platoon, Mario made the same choice.

Even though Samuel and Mario never went to Vietnam or fought alongside the U.S. Air Force, Samuel felt like a true Peruvian American. It was during this time that his love and admiration for America earned him the lifelong nickname: "Tio Sam," or Uncle Sam. Samuel promised himself that one day, somehow, he would visit the Land of the Brave.

At the conclusion of his military service in Lima, Samuel returned to Arequipa to work as a mechanic and driver at the bus company. One day, he stumbled upon the rusted shell of a Willys Jeep in an abandoned vehicle lot. Despite its damaged engine, lack of windows, and missing tires, something about it captivated him. Samuel contacted the lot owner and purchased the dilapidated vehicle for a negligible sum. Over the next several months, he and his buddies, went to work on the piece of junk he had purchased. With their mechanical skills, the parts that Samuel ordered from Lima, and countless hours of labor, they transformed it into a respectable "military" Jeep, allowing him to drive around town with Betty and hang out with his friends.

Samuel cherished that Willys Jeep for years. He had learned from the lot owner that the Jeep had originally been part of the U.S. military's post-World War II aid to the allied nations. The Peruvian Army had utilized it before dismantling it for spare parts. To Tio Sam, that Jeep held value that transcended its age. It was a tangible symbol of his twin passions: owning a piece of esteemed American military equipment and embodying the American Dream in Peru. Every time Samuel tinkered with the Jeep or took it out for a spin, he felt transported into the realm of classic war films, envisioning himself as John Wayne or in later years, reliving scenes reminiscent of M.A.S.H. alongside his mechanic buddies. The Jeep became a source of immense pride and joy, encapsulating his admiration for American culture and his own aspirations.

Passing on the Dream

In the 1960s, the growing influence of the Soviet-Cuban alliance stoked fears that communism would spread into South America, causing the United States to intensify efforts to maintain control of the region. The once friendly, albeit unequal and awkward, commercial relations between Peru and the U.S. turned increasingly imperialistic by the mid-1960s.[8] U.S. meddling in the internal affairs of Peru (and in those of most nations in the Western hemisphere) provoked strong reactions, especially from the traditional center and left-of-center political sectors of Peruvian society.

Peru faced significant challenges, including poverty, economic disparities, and a fragile democracy debilitated by foreign intervention seeking control over its natural resources. By 1968, halfway through the administration of President Fernando Belaunde Terry, a highly educated and respected scholar, Peru was in a deep socio-political crisis, with discontent on two fronts: land problems postponed since colonial times and grotesque foreign meddling by multinational oil and mineral extraction companies in domestic policies that affected the economy.

Despite efforts to combat foreign corporate greed and boost state revenue for development, President Belaunde Terry's administration was stymied by corruption and scandals. An infamous scandal surfaced involving the missing "Page 11" of a 1968 oil contract, known as the Talara Act, which was meant to resolve an 80-year tax evasion and land rights dispute with the U.S.-based International Petroleum Company in Peru's Northeast region. Shortly after signing, investigations revealed the absence of Page 11, which allegedly detailed millions of dollars in benefits to the oil company, paid for by the Peruvian people. Social and political unrest escalated as Belaunde's administration faced

---

[8] See Dependency, Liberty and Equity, and Post-dependency Frameworks in the Bibliography section for additional information on the complex relationships between the U.S. and Latin American nations.

accusations of further enabling foreign violations of Peruvian sovereignty.

The pendulum had swung too far toward the foreign intervention side, creating incredible momentum that swung it back in the opposite direction toward another extreme: nationalism. Widespread feelings of indignation had paved the way for the emergence of a nationalist dictator. Capitalizing on the social discontent, General Juan Velasco Alvarado orchestrated a military coup that resulted in the ousting of President Belaunde Terry. In exile, the former Peruvian president found ready sanctuary in the United States and even assumed teaching positions at Harvard and Columbia Universities. With President Belaunde Terry gone, General Velasco's regime aimed to restore order and reclaim Peru's sovereignty by addressing the issues of corruption and the breaches of sovereignty prevalent during President Belaunde Terry's democratic rule.

Despite heightened tensions between Peru and the U.S., certain American programs remained, including President Kennedy's Alliance for Progress,[9] which later became part of the U.S. Agency for International Development (USAID). Peru also maintained its membership in key international financial institutions like the World Bank, the International Monetary Fund, and the Inter-American Development Bank. In conjunction with the U.S.-led Alliance for Progress, public schools implemented breakfast programs to combat

---

[9] Alliance for Progress was a U.S. initiative launched in 1961, aimed at fostering economic cooperation and development in Latin America. It sought to counteract the spread of communism by promoting social reform, economic modernization, and democratic governance in the region. The program included financial aid, technical assistance, and efforts to improve education, health care, and housing.

malnutrition among students, often serving as the sole source of sustenance for many children across the nation.

The military government of General Velasco Alvarado (1968-1975) wanted to distance Peru from the ideological polarization of the Cold War and focus on the social and economic needs of Peruvians. General Velasco nationalized the oil industry and other key sectors, which increased economic austerity. However, his military-style discipline kept the peace in the country and shaped the 1970s in Peru.

My childhood was marked by city-wide curfews, mandated school uniforms, and strict respect for teachers and authorities. In school, physical education was combined with pre-military training, and military-style haircuts were very much in style. Perhaps because we lived under a military regime and civil liberties were limited, most Peruvians were unaware that General Velasco was actually trying to prepare Peru to go to war against Chile by 1979 (the 100th anniversary of the Pacific War[10]) to recover the two states it had lost in that war—Arica and Iquique.

During the Velasco military regime, Hollywood movies were largely banned, except for war movies (mostly about WWII) and cowboy movies. General Velasco likely believed that those films would encourage aggressive, militaristic, macho behavior among Peruvians, which would be advantageous for his intentions to confront Chile.

---

[10] The Pacific War (1879-1884) was fought between Chile and the alliance of Peru and Bolivia over territorial disputes, particularly control of nitrate-rich areas. Chile emerged victorious, seizing land from both. England supported Chile diplomatically and economically, providing loans and naval aid. Britain's interest was driven by access to Peru's valuable guano and nitrate resources, crucial for agricultural fertilizers and industrial use.

Meanwhile in Chile, General Augusto Pinochet, supported by the U.S. Central Intelligence Agency (CIA), removed and killed that country's elected socialist president, Salvador Allende, in 1973. Pinochet had his own war plans, which caused Chile and Peru to enter into an arms race, complete with Cold-War style espionage activities. Consequently, both countries began allocating much-needed social financial resources into weaponry purchases from rich industrialized nations.

In Peru, General Velasco's plans were derailed in 1975, when he was deposed from power in a coup d'état led by General Francisco Morales Bermúdez, a right-leaning military leader. Soon after coming to power, General Morales Bermúdez joined *Plan Condor,* a CIA-backed effort to stop socialist and communist leaders from gaining power in South America. Morales Bermudez succeeded in discrediting his predecessor and undoing key reforms that Velasco had put into place, paving the way for a democratic return to power for President Belaunde Terry, who began his second term in 1980.

With President Belaunde Terry back in power, Peru witnessed the resurgence of international lobbies, accompanied by the revival of powerful special interests. In an effort to promote more balanced economic and political progress in Peru, Belaunde Terry brought in U.S.-trained economists influenced by neoliberal policies, like those in Pinochet's Chile, to reform the economy. However, the economic model, similar to those in Margaret Thatcher's Britain and Ronald Reagan's America, was poorly suited for Peru's unique circumstances and proved ineffective. With the gradual influx of international corporations, Peruvians' way of life underwent significant changes as local industries collapsed and creativity was stifled. By 1984, guerrilla movements such as the Shining Path had gained significant power and momentum in the absence of "strong-hand" style military governments.

With President Belaunde Terry's return, addictive foreign TV programming (and advertisements) also made a comeback, despite the precarious financial situation of most Peruvians. "The more TV sets in Peruvian homes, the more consumers," seemed to have been the economic mantra of the time. Somehow, even some of the poorest people managed to borrow money to buy a television set, sometimes using their homes as collateral. Perhaps they were just desperate to escape the hard but true economic reality of Peru in the 1980s.

From TV to Reality

Prior to television, life was simple. I had lots of friends and lived in a loving community that was undisturbed by cars, technology, or pressure to buy the latest products. I never thought of myself as "poor." In fact, I never even thought about money at all. I was much more interested in running around barefoot in my neighborhood and playing with my friends. Rocks, sticks, and recyclable cans or boxes were our favorite "toys" throughout my childhood. Technicolor television sets had started appearing in more and more of my neighbors' homes, however, and eventually, my parents managed to buy one for us.

Having access to television was a turning point in my life. As I began to watch TV shows and commercials from Lima,

Argentina, Mexico, and the U.S., I discovered how much was "missing" in my life. Watching kids and their families playing with cool toys we couldn't afford and traveling to exotic places, made me realize how poor we were compared to those who "had it all." I began to feel ashamed of my beat-up shoes and the patched and repatched clothes I wore. They were symbols of our poverty, and poverty had become "bad." My siblings and I began to beg our parents for things they couldn't afford. Family arguments and resentments increased due to what we now perceived as our unmet "needs."

Having a TV set was still a luxury for most people, however. Those who were lucky enough to own one had to make their homes more secure. Television sets became the number one attraction for robbers, and break-ins were common in homes that had televisions. Many neighborhoods became unsafe, and people began to fear strangers. Like other TV owners, we lined the walls of our home with cemented-in shards of broken glass and small cactus branches to protect it from would-be robbers who might climb them to gain entry. Some of our neighbors installed metal doors and barbed wire along the edges of their roofs.

International TV networks provided fresh news about what was happening in the United States and in Europe. We didn't hear much about any other continent; in our eyes, the U.S. was the world outside Peru. American events such as the landing on the moon and the legacies of Dr. Martin Luther King Jr. and John F. Kennedy were passed down via radio and television programming and kept in the collective memory, a phenomenon sometimes called *remote acculturation*.[11] Peruvian streets, schools, and institutions were named after Dr. King, Kennedy, Roosevelt, and other European or U.S. presidents or leaders. I have remote acculturation to thank for my nickname, "El Chino" (the Chinese man). El Chino was Charles Bronson's nickname in one of his movies, and my eyes and attitude reminded my friends of Bronson. I must admit it felt good to be associated with a brave American actor whose characters fought and beat the bad guys in Western movies or caught criminals in the streets of New York City.

By 1984, my last year of high school, breakdancing was all the rage among young Peruvians. Despite living in a dusty shantytown, my friends and I practiced our breakdancing moves wherever we could find a smooth concrete floor. When Michael Jackson's *Thriller* hit Peru, my friends and I began wearing dark-colored pants, white socks, and synthetic jackets. Some of my friends even tried to curl their hair! Kids and teens imitated Michael at school performances, family parties, and on street corners.[12] We loved

---

[11] Remote acculturation refers to unidirectional influence, generally from industrialized to developing nations, via radio, television, film, and entertainment. This influence occurs by transmitting narratives and cultural products, such as lifestyles, fashion, languages, behaviors, and values, from one country to another, leading to their adoption as they blend with the recipient nation's own traditions. Sometimes, this occurs at the expense of the original cultural identity.

[12] Admiration or fascination were a natural reaction of Peruvian youth to American influences. Lawrence Clayton (1999) explains this phenomenon, where Peruvians seem to alternatively view the United States with both reverence and suspicion or dislike. Additional theories that describe the nature of relations between the U.S. and Latin America can be found in the Bibliography section.

Michael so much that we officially named our class the "Michael Jackson Class of 1984."

When the news about our official class name made it to the local newspaper, it didn't go over well with our elders. The newspaper published a scathing OpEd in which the author complained bitterly about "how brain-washed our youth have become," and how Peruvians no longer love their Peruvian identity or ethnic heritage. My teenage self didn't get it at the time, but the author had a good point. The fact was (and still is) that America and American culture was so ingrained in the subconscious minds of Peruvians (including my family and I) that we didn't even notice it had happened

Handing Out Aid and Ideology

President Kennedy's Alliance for Progress program continued in Peru until the 2000s under USAID. Alliance for Progress provided basic food items such as rice, sugar, soybeans, cooking oil, and non-perishable canned goods to help developing countries. It was special in that it gave assistance to communities involved in projects that directly benefited the poor. Alliance for Progress worked primarily with grassroot organizations, non-governmental organizations (NGOs), and faith-based organizations, not government agencies (mainly to avoid red tape and corruption). In our neighborhood, Alliance for Progress supported the construction of our neighborhood chapel. With the help of a German priest, people in our community formed a committee and formally asked for help from the Alliance program. For 15 months, many families worked on weekends to build the church, digging holes and carrying bricks. A paid crew also worked during the week. The committee tracked who helped, and every two weeks, those families got food from the Alliance program based on their service. When it was finally finished, the church was the biggest building in our community, with a community center, classrooms, and rooms for three nuns, two of whom were American.

Alliance for Progress symbolized both our community's collective spirit and Kennedy's impact on Peru. Implemented in impoverished regions across the country, the initiative reflected Kennedy's widely accepted foreign policy in Latin America, which was embraced particularly by marginalized populations. Kennedy's enduring legacy among the poor persisted for decades after his passing, representing hope for international friendship amid the challenges of the Cold War era. Certain sectors of Peruvian society, however, particularly some political party leaders, perceived Kennedy's program as just one more flavor of U.S. intervention in Peru's internal affairs. Communist movements like the Shining Path condemned Alliance for Progress as a tool for the U.S. to spread propaganda among Peru's vulnerable populations and influence their allegiance. To them, the program existed only to promote imperialism and dependency.

Whether intentional or not, the fact was that although it provided essential food to those in need, Alliance for Progress did not address the root causes of poverty. Rather than taking significant steps to lift people out of poverty, the initiative reinforced the stereotype—instilled by television and government authorities—that indigenous and *mestizo* individuals were inherently poor and in need of charity. The subtle but impactful message was that impoverished Peruvians couldn't control their destinies and required aid from governments, NGOs, or international organizations. This insidious belief, nurtured by three centuries of Spanish colonial conditioning, continued to flourish in the collective Peruvian consciousness.

To provide some context, consider that when Peru gained its independence in 1821, its white minority ruling class continued to propagate oppressive policies and narratives in the country, despite the fact that the population was 90 percent indigenous and *mestizo*.[13] Shortly thereafter, the United States became a world superpower, and a new, more subtle form of foreign interventionism continued to support the same narrative in Peru (and the Western hemisphere), reinforcing the idea that individuals of European decent were inherently superior to those with dark skin. Most Peruvians have historically accepted and embraced foreign lifestyles, religions, and charity because of their lack of authentic independence. This state of dependence on international corporations, however, has also planted seeds in the unconscious collective for a culture of emigration to the United States and elsewhere.

---

[13] In Peru, segregation policies, land dispossession, and discriminatory laws against indigenous communities continued well into the 20th century. While slavery was abolished in 1854, the "Hacendado" practice, which permitted landlords to own entire villages or towns, continued to exist as a form of quasi-slavery until 1969. Indigenous spiritual practices are still marginalized and unprotected.

Photo 1. My father during parachute training in the Peruvian Air Force in the early 1960s.

CHAPTER 2

The Peruvian Dream Is Over

"In the end, it's not the years in your life that count.
It's the life in your years."

~ Abraham Lincoln

As December of 1984 unfolded, I stood on the precipice of my high school graduation, oblivious to the turbulent reality awaiting me. The Belaunde administration was in its final year, and the economy was in a downward spiral on its way toward a total collapse. Peru's economy had dwindled to depths unseen in four decades, a stark contrast to the relative stability of the previous 12 years of military rule. As the economic woes intensified, union strikes became commonplace, and the specter of insurgent attacks loomed over the nation. Unemployment surged, prompting a wave of emigration to industrialized countries as people sought refuge from the unraveling socioeconomic fabric. Many talented scientists, engineers, or other highly qualified individuals were unable to find opportunities in Peru, which forced them to emigrate to other countries, intensifying the "brain drain" phenomenon.

I watched as my family's financial stability crumbled before our eyes. The cozy convenience store that my mom had run for years had to close its doors. The paycheck from my dad's full-time job as a driver for a local bank wasn't enough to cover our needs. There were times when things as basic as toilet paper became unaffordable. Meat, once a staple on our plates, vanished due to its soaring cost. We became vigilant about our water and electricity usage, scaling back to keep the bills at bay. But it still wasn't enough. To make ends meet, my dad took on a second job as a taxi driver, tacking on another 4-6 hours to his already full workday. My parents argued constantly over money, and our home was transformed into a battleground where every decision revolved around stretching our limited resources. Financial hardship reshaped every aspect of our lives.

As the countdown to my graduation day ticked away, a surge of anxiety gripped me, casting a shadow of uncertainty over my future. The only thing I knew for sure was that I was not equipped to navigate a society in freefall. As the world around me succumbed to economic strife, political unrest, and the resurgence of a guerrilla menace, the stark truth emerged—the skills to confront and navigate a society in ruins were conspicuously absent from my educational toolkit.

As I considered my limited options, one glimmer of hope emerged—a coveted spot at the sole public university in town. With unwavering determination, I confidently proclaimed to anyone who asked that I was going to study civil engineering so I could start my own construction company.

My daydreams were filled with engineers in bright yellow hardhats huddled over floor plans, gesturing towards sleek, modern structures and bridges. In the world of civil engineering, I could combine my passion for drawing and love of intricate design with the technical prowess I would gain through my studies. The prospect of crafting sophisticated blueprints beckoned as the logical evolution of my skills.

After graduation, I devoted all my time to preparing for the college admissions exam. Passing that exam was the only way to get into the university, and the exam was only held once a year. There were around 30,000 applicants, but only 2,200 spaces were available, so the competition was fierce. In my field, the competition was even stiffer. There were 2,000 applicants competing for just 35 available spots in the civil engineering school. For 4 months, I studied at home and in the city library to get ready for the exam.

My nerves were on overdrive during the entire 3-hour exam, and when it was finally over, I went home exhausted and hungry. I wanted to be alone until the results were broadcast on the local radio station. That night, my entire family was glued to the boombox radio on the kitchen table. The announcer read the results alphabetically, school by school. When I heard, "… admitted to the School of Civil Engineering, in alphabetic order…," my heart started to race. My eyes focused on the round speakers of the boombox like lasers.

There were only two last names that started with an "S," and neither was "Sánchez." *Something must have happened, there must be a mistake!* I was in shock. I picked up the boombox and shook it in disbelief, as if that would somehow make the speakers spit out "Ricardo Sánchez." I could not believe what was happening. My parents and siblings tried to console me as I broke down in tears. My only opportunity to receive higher education had disappeared like a bubble that popped without warning; it was one of the darkest moments in my life.

The next day, I went to the university to look at the lists of applicants and admittances posted on the wall. What I saw on that wall cut me to the core. I was number 36 on the list. I'd literally missed being accepted by less than one point! But the harsh reality was that it didn't matter. I may have been next in line, but my score wasn't good enough. I didn't make it.

During the next 2 weeks, I couldn't sleep. I kept thinking, something is going to happen. Surely, one of the thirty-five students that had passed the exam would drop out, and I would be admitted. I visited the admissions office several times, checking again and again to see if someone had dropped. I was about to turn seventeen and already, I felt like the biggest failure, just another statistic in the growing jobless population. I couldn't accept the thought of being a burden on my impoverished family, not when I had 5 younger siblings looking up to me.

Every morning, I left the house early so that I wouldn't eat the food that my younger siblings needed. I stayed out on the streets all day, looking for work that would pay at least enough for a meal. With no work experience of any kind, I sat in various plazas and parks and read the classified ads, trying to find a job, any job. But call after call ended the same way: "Sorry, the position is already taken." Sometimes, I learned, the people who were hired were so desperate that they almost worked for free.

Weeks after my failed attempt to enter college, I had another crazy idea. Growing up, I'd heard many stories from my dad about how he and 'Uncle' Mario had almost volunteered for the Vietnam War while serving in the Air Force. As a child, I'd dreamt of being a pilot in the Escuela de Oficiales de la Fuerza Aérea del Perú (Peruvian Air Force Officers Academy). As a pilot, I'd get to fly fast American aircraft like the robust Herks that my dad had always talked about. It was a crazy dream, though, because there were many daunting hurdles that I'd have to jump over to get a foot in the door, starting with the fact that we lived in Arequipa, which was a 16-hour drive from Lima, the Peruvian capital. In my highly centralized country, Lima was where everything happened; it was the center of politics, the economy, health, education, wealth, news, and, of course, the military.

I transformed my daily routine into a rigorous regimen, complete with morning runs, swimming sessions, and relentless athletic drills, and I was equally relentless in my attempts to convince my parents to let me apply to the Academy. My naïve mind convinced me that if I tried hard enough, maybe I'd have a shot at getting in. The sheer audacity of my ambition stemmed from the Academy's exclusive nature. Given its exorbitant entrance fee, the Academy was primarily reserved for the privileged few, those with familial ties or influential connections, and I had none of those. We were not part of the Peruvian elite socioeconomic class, had no connections in Lima, and certainly could not afford to pay the entrance fee. But I was desperate, so I ignored these stark truths and continued pressuring my parents to let me apply.

Fed up and at his wits end, my dad finally called Uncle Mario and put me on the line. Uncle Mario knew the ins and outs of how the admissions system worked, and he was brutally honest as he told me the hard reality of Peru in 1985. The Academy was not designed for the best candidates, even those with superior physical and intellectual abilities, he told me. Rather, it was for those with good connections, and it was rife with racism and nepotism at the highest levels. Well-connected white Limeños (people from Lima) had a huge advantage over brown provincianos (people from the provinces). Even the few who got perfect scores according to the admissions criteria got "pushed down" to make room for those who were better connected, both during the admissions process and later, in their career advancement. I listened to Uncle Mario with growing resentment—not toward him but toward the inequalities in the system and the lack of opportunities in Peru. The grotesque injustice in Peru was, and still is, the biggest impediment to both economic and human development.

The doors to my two biggest dreams had been slammed shut, and there was nothing I could do about it. Deprived of the chance to pursue any of my goals, I resigned myself to doing whatever temporary jobs I could find. Like millions of other Peruvians, I began living a life with no dreams, working for pennies. I gave the little bit of money that I made doing odd jobs to my parents to help them buy notebooks, clothes, and shoes for my younger siblings. Now, my only goal was just not to be a burden on my family or use resources that my parents needed for my 5 younger siblings, who ranged in age from 5 to 15 years old.

A Surprise Visit During Cloudy Days

The weeks passed, adding layer upon layer of pessimism to my feelings of impotence about the depressing situation in Peru. Sunday afternoons were the worst. I felt numb, and daydreaming was my only relief as I tried to avoid my compulsion to perform a mental status check to gauge how much higher my pile of broken dreams had grown with each passing week. Nagging thoughts of never becoming an air force pilot or a civil engineer stole my self-confidence and shook my entire being.

The arrival of each new Monday felt like one of those nightmares where you see the train coming that you are supposed to board, but a powerful force pulls you down and you can't move. And before you can escape that force, the train departs, leaving you behind forever. At 17, with nothing but a high school diploma, I felt stuck, trapped, depressed, and totally devoid of hope. Often, I hung with other unemployed young adults on the street corner. If I had earned a few coins doing odd jobs the week before, I sometimes played poker on the street corners, both to pass the time and in the hopes of "earning" some cash to bring home. I wasn't really there to play poker, though. I sat on the street corner to signal that I was an active day laborer, waiting to do chores for anyone who had the means to hire me for a few hours.

On one melancholic Sunday, the sound of someone knocking on the front door startled me out of my funk. My siblings ran to the window to see who it was. "Aunt Juana!!" They yelled. She had come from the U.S. for one of her occasional visits. In our minds, she came from another world—a world where everything was happy and there was abundance everywhere. Although her visits only lasted a couple of hours, each time she came, her memories and anecdotes became topics of family conversation all year long. Her face was like that of a baby doll, with a big smile from cheek to cheek. She was always happy, and she wore colorful outfits, like most American tourists. Before opening the door, we all ran to put on our flip flops, comb our hair, change out of our dirty t-shirts, and clean up the living room in 60 seconds flat. It was our way of showing Aunt Juana that although we were poor, we cared about her and honored her visits. I was the last one to run to the door because I didn't want to be disturbed from my depressed state. But when I heard it was Aunt Juana, I immediately suspended my melancholic Sunday afternoon mood and joined my siblings in the crazy race to get ready for her.

Tio Sam and Mama Betty happily greeted Aunt Juana, encouraging all seven of us kids to hug and kiss our gringa Aunt. She and my father had been close since childhood, when they both had migrated from the Valley of Volcanoes. My dad and Aunt Juana always teased each other, and they often added in Quechua words, which made the two of them continue giggling long after the rest of us had stopped laughing. Only they could understand the extra spin that Quechua added to their jokes. This time, Aunt Juana threw some English words into the mix, not to be funny but to add some nuance to the idea she wanted to communicate. Every time she snuck in an English word, though, it had the opposite effect on us. We stopped paying attention to her sentence and became intrigued by the new fancy word, and we asked her to teach us some English words.

It wasn't just the new English words that made this visit different from all the previous ones. It was the dismal state of Peru and my own state of mind. Unlike other years, this time, part of me wished I was in her shoes. I wanted to be the one who traveled from a faraway place to visit my relatives and be seen as "accomplished." Aunt Juana was one of only a few relatives who had "made it" in our eyes because she had escaped the problems of life in Peru. To us, she was living the American Dream, and for the first time, I envied her.

That afternoon, we went with Aunt Juana to a traditional restaurant for a rare meal out, and we took full advantage of the chance to eat meat. Meat had become unusual in our diet because we simply couldn't afford it. But that day, we ate like kings and had fun as my parents and Aunt Juana reminisced about old times. When the check landed on the table in front of my dad, I got a glimpse of the total and was taken aback— $189 Intis (the former Peruvian currency), which was equivalent to $14 U.S. dollars! It was an exorbitant amount of money by Peruvian standards.[1] Despite my dad's poker face, I could sense his shock. He held the check and reached for his wallet, but I knew he didn't have even a fraction of that amount. Nevertheless, he tried to shrug off his concern with a classic "no worries, it's on me" gesture. Aunt Juana, knowing our situation only too well, swiftly intervened, saying, "Don't worry, hermanito (little brother), I'll pay." My father

---

[1] In 1985, Peru used the Inti as its currency. The Inti was replaced by the Nuevo Sol (PEN) in 1991 due to hyperinflation (inflation rates reached 7,650% in 1990). In 1985, the minimum wage was approximately 1,700 Intis per month. By the late 1980s, inflation had eroded the purchasing power of the Inti, meaning that 1,700 Intis were worth much less in real terms.

feigned reluctance, saying, "No, no, I'll pay," but it was clear he couldn't. After a brief back-and-forth, Aunt Juana prevailed. Despite my father's chagrin, I could tell he was secretly relieved. Aunt Juana asked the waiter, "Can I pay with U.S. dollars?" "Of course, ma'am," the waiter replied.

Aunt Juana grabbed her imitation Louis Vuitton purse and paid the tab for our feast. I was struck by both the amount of money she had just paid and the ease with which it was done. Then, she gave each of us presents. Mine was a purple T-shirt with a drawing of the U.S. Capitol and the words, "Washington, D.C." Aunt Juana told us how beautiful, advanced, and organized the United States was. She said that she lived in a mansion and drove her own car. My mind assumed that Aunt Juana must enjoy a lifestyle like the characters on the American prime time television soap opera "Dallas," which aired in Peru from 1978 to 1991. The series was filled with the dramas of the affluent, feuding Texas family, the Ewings, who owned their own independent oil company and a cattle ranch called Southfork. *My aunt is rich,* I said to myself, *very rich.* She left us at the restaurant shortly after handing out her gifts and returned to the U.S. a few days later, leaving us wondering when we would get to see her again.

All too soon, it was Monday again. I worked on and off as a helper for a local carpenter but barely made enough to pay for my own food, let alone have any leftover money to help my parents make ends meet. I wished I could contribute more because I hated seeing my siblings go to school with "ventilated" (i.e., holey) shoes, as we used to joke. *My older brother was so lucky to have gotten into medical school,* I thought. He had to study his medical textbooks by candlelight because we couldn't pay the electric bills; and even when we managed to make the odd payment, there were strict government rations on energy use.

Amidst Peru's worsening economic conditions, the 1985 election campaign became a breeding ground for populist candidates who offered promises of relief for the poor and a full economic turnaround. The electorate, yearning for a change in the nation's trajectory, ultimately chose Alan Garcia Perez—a young lawyer with a left-center political ideology, who had mastered the art of public speaking. Despite Garcia Perez' grandiose promises to address the injustices and all the plans and proposals he so skillfully articulated, his administration was filled with corrupt officials and hidden personal agendas. Instead of improving Peruvians' lives, things got even worse. Within a year of Garcia's coming into power, the country was officially in a deep economic depression. One day, the Garcia administration decided to stop sending payments to international financial lending institutions such as the World Bank and International Monetary Fund (IMF). This decision led to retaliation by the Washington Consensus (i.e., the IMF, the World Bank, and the U.S. Department of Treasury). Their retaliation consisted of a total isolation of Peru from the financial markets, which sent the country into even more financial chaos.

The Garcia administration tried to use the cash it had "saved" by not repaying Peru's international loans to lend money to small businesses, farmers, and entrepreneurs, encouraging them to start new businesses with low or zero-interest loans. It also used some of the money to invest in education and pay for scholarships to send some students to study abroad. But the unplanned transition to a nationalistic economy, with no financial structure or support, did not produce the results Garcia had hoped for. Corruption among special interests and Lima's elite, along with systemic racism and greed, led to the collapse of Garcia's plan. Within a year, most of the businesses that had borrowed money from the government defaulted on their payments, and many declared bankruptcy. To make matters worse; investors, the few remaining big businesses, and corrupt politicians transferred all their money—much of it stolen from the government—to offshore accounts, depleting the Peruvian financial system. It was the biggest embezzlement of money from the Peruvian state in history.

The already weak economy went into a tailspin in 1986, and hyperinflation ran wild, reaching 114.5% per year, with over 15% unemployment.[2] The prices of gas and basic food items could barely keep up with the inflation rate, jumping 30% to 40% per month. Meanwhile, the communist ideologues in the Shining Path movement capitalized on the general chaos, calling for a violent takeover of the Peruvian state. Massacres by both guerrillas and the Peruvian armed forces became normal topics in the evening news. Not a day went by without yet another heinous act of terrorism. The daily news broadcasts became a never-ending series of reports on all the people who had died that day in explosions in the business districts and all the electrical towers that had been destroyed in the cities and towns. indigenous villages

---

[2] This figure does not fully capture the extent of the economic crisis, as underemployment (people working fewer hours than they would like or in jobs that did not utilize their skills) was also a significant issue. Approximately 65% of Peruvian labor force engaged in the informal economy due to the lack of formal employment opportunities.

were burned and indigenous people who refused to join the guerrilla movement were massacred by the hundreds or thousands. There were also reports of massacrers committed by the Peruvian army.

A documentary that I watched in the summer of 1986 shocked me even more than all the news reports in Peru. It was about El Salvador and the Salvadoran children who had been forced to join the rebel forces to fight in the Salvadoran Civil War. Ten-year-old orphans who had lost their parents to the Salvadoran army were being trained and were chanting about revenge. It scared me to see how full-scale civil wars had broken out in other Latin American nations, and I feared that the same thing would happen in Peru. I saw my younger siblings in the faces of those Salvadoran children, and I felt increasingly responsible for my family's safety and well-being. Like millions of impoverished, unemployed, indignant Peruvians, I participated in street demonstrations to protest the lack of basic services and jobs and the exorbitant prices for basic food items, fuel, and other necessities. Yet despite all the fear and hardships, I was still a teenager trying to find my place in the community and in society at large.

I once had a dream that I was flying high in the skies as a pilot in an Air Force jet. Then, suddenly, my plane had zero fuel and began to fall from the sky. I freaked out and awoke with my heart pounding. I spent countless sleepless nights thinking about my future. In desperation, I often looked up at the sky and asked, "*¿Que será de mi?*" ("What will become of me?") One day, after posing that question yet again, a light of hope began to flicker unexpectedly in my mind like a message surfacing from the deepest of places: *Go to America! Go to America!*

I had just watched the film *E.T.* and I felt as if I was the extra-terrestrial. I was the creature pointing to a faraway planet, saying "E.T., phone home!" An alien longing to go home to… America. It took me a few months to convince myself that this crazy idea of migrating to America might actually be possible. But the more I thought about it, the more real it became. I had heard that the minimum wage in the U.S. was $3.35 per hour. By my calculations, that meant $26.80 per day, or $536 per month. That was half of what my dad earned in one year! I figured that if I stayed at Aunt Juana's mansion, I wouldn't have pay much for room and board. That way, I'd be able to save money to help my family. And maybe I could even go to college at night. I started doing a little research and soon learned that specialized laborers were better paid, as much as $10 or $15 per hour! *I must learn a trade before I go*, I thought.

When I finally got up the courage to tell my parents about my decision, my dad told me flat out: "No!" It was crazy to think I could get a visa, he told me, let alone be able to pay over a thousand dollars for travel expenses. "Aunt Juana has enough problems and responsibilities to deal with," he told me. "The last thing she needs is another person to worry about and feel responsible for. Plus, you don't speak English, and she would have to be your translator, too. You know nothing about the way of life in America!" "No way," said my mother, adding her voice to my father's objections. "What if they don't give you a visa? The fees for visa applications are non-refundable; and a lot of money would go to waste!" And the list went on and on. Of course, there was another unspoken reason why they did not want me to migrate. Their 17-year-old boy would be gone, and the family would be separated indefinitely. They might not ever see me again. But my mind was made up. My poorly paying job at the furniture factory wasn't going to teach me anything. I kept bringing the topic up, week after week, whenever I had a chance.

Preparing for Take-Off

The journey of 4,000 miles starts with a tourist visa. It took months of relentless assault, but either my parents got tired of my stubbornness, or my arguments to migrate to America began to make sense to them. Whatever the reason, they finally relented and began to take my plan seriously.

We figured it would take at least seven months to save enough money to apply for a Peruvian passport and be ready to submit a visa application. First, I had to get my Peruvian adult identification card, school transcripts, health records, and police records. Each of these processes took between two and six weeks, and we had to pay processing fees for each. Only with all these in hand could I formally request a passport. The last step was to travel to Lima for the in-person application and interview process at the U.S. Embassy, which required paying a non-refundable fee of $95. To be accepted for a tourist visa, I would have to show that I had enough money to cover my travel expenses in the U.S., including the costs of the airplane tickets and my room and board for at least a couple of months. We knew it would be a very expensive endeavor, but we also felt that it would be well worth it.

My father agreed that learning a specialized trade before going to the U.S. was a good idea, since it would enable me to find a job that paid more than minimum wage. However, we couldn't afford to pay for formal training, so he suggested that I try to learn by working as a *chuli*, or helper. Because no one was hiring, my only option was to offer to work for free in return for a chance to gain experience. *What if I learned how to fix cars? I bet I could make a lot of money by working as a mechanic in America,* I thought. So, I went out to look for auto repair shops willing to have me as a helper.

After knocking on a few doors, I found a car repair shop that agreed to let me work for free. I didn't last more than three weeks at the place, though. There were too many issues with the owner of the shop. Some days, he showed up at work drunk and verbally mistreated everyone. Then, he was caught cheating a bunch of customers, and one day, a group of angry customers came to the shop and tried to beat him up when he refused to give them back their money. I had had enough of that toxic environment, so I gathered my tools and left for good.

The following week, I went to visit my old boss, Mr. Romero, who owned a furniture factory. During my pre-teen years, I had worked there over the summers, cleaning the sawdust and wood shavings. This time, I asked Mr. Romero if he would let me be the woodcarver's helper and clean the factory, all for free. I told Mr. Romero that I wanted to become a woodcarver. Getting on-the-job training was the only way I could get hands-on experience, since there were no woodcarving schools in Peru. The woodcarving trade was largely passed down from one generation to the next in Peru, except for a few exceptional woodcarvers who managed to teach themselves.

"Why do you want to become a wood carver?" Mr. Romero asked. "You are young; you should go to college. Woodcarving is an old man's job. It's only for those who don't go to school."

I didn't tell him the real reason, I only said that I was interested in learning the art and I really wanted to become a good woodcarver. "Woodcarving is a seasonal job," he warned. "Some weeks, there is not enough business to keep all the woodcarvers on staff. That's why they only get paid per item that they finish. They don't earn hourly or monthly salaries." I noticed Mr. Romero's hesitation and knew that it came, in part, because many woodcarvers misspent their money on alcohol. When I continued to persist, Mr. Romero finally said, "Ok, you can come and work next Monday, if it's ok with Señor Bigotes. He is good when he is sober," he said. "But don't say I didn't warn you if you become a drunkard like him," he added, only half joking. "Just make sure the factory stays clean."

Señor Bigotes was in his early thirties. He was single, and he lived in a rented room near my parents' house. After paying the fee for his *pensión* (boarding house),[3] which covered his daily meals, he spent the rest of his money on liquor, which he drank with his alcoholic friends. Even though he was usually still drunk when he showed up for work on Monday mornings, he was such a good carver that even in his half-drunk state, he managed to use the right chisels and hit the mallet with just the right amount of force to achieve the desired effect in the wood.

---

[3] As used in this context, "pensión" refers to a small boarding house or guesthouse that offers lodging, often with meals.

I met Señor Bigotes on a Monday morning, which was a good thing because he was still in a good mood despite his hangover. He accepted my offer to be his volunteer helper, much to my relief. My main job was to line up all the chairs and furniture and trace outlines of 16th century French designs in pencil on the wood surfaces to guide him in his carving. Señor Bigotes was a *mestizo* who had migrated years earlier from the highlands to Arequipa. His mustache was huge by Peruvian standards, and that's why his friends called him "Señor Bigotes" (Mr. Mustache). He had been working in the factory for about three years, and despite his usual Monday hangovers and occasional tardiness, he was never fired because he was the best woodcarver on the staff.

As the weeks went by, I began to learn the art of woodcarving. I must have had some talent because after a few weeks of working for free, Mr. Romero surprised me by paying me along with the other workers. Bigotes was sometimes impatient with me, but overall, we got along fine. After four months, I began to notice that he still wasn't letting me carve very often. He made up excuses to keep me from doing the nicer designs. By this time, I had bought myself a set of carving chisels so he wouldn't be bothered by me using his tools, but that didn't help.

One chilly winter Monday, Bigotes showed up to work three hours late. Mr. Romero's patience was thin, and as soon as Bigotes entered the shop, he yelled at Bigotes for being late and hungover again. Mr. Romero had a bad habit of ridiculing his employees in front of everyone whenever he noticed that one of them had made furniture that was a bit crooked, or if he caught them slacking. This time, Bigotes was the target of Mr. Romero's ridicule. "Well, well, well!

Look who just came into the shop, CEO Bigotes! He shows up to work whenever he pleases and doesn't give a shit about finishing the furniture or meeting deadlines. And on top of that, he has the balls to ask for a raise! Let's give him a round of applause, shall we?" Bigotes looked embarrassed and ashamed as he walked in the direction of his work bench. Obviously, no one applauded. Everyone knew it was just Mr. Romero's way to use sarcasm to put Bigotes in his place. Hiding his anger, Bigotes said, "I am sorry, Boss, it is not going to happen again."

Mr. Romero's humiliating and harsh verbal punishment highlighted the stark contrast between Bigotes and himself. As the owner of the carpentry shop, Mr. Romero was a true and committed entrepreneur who led by example. He was never late with pay days and he looked after the wellbeing of the families of each employee, all while managing every aspect of the business during a time when most businesses had collapsed. He was well respected for keeping his word, and he was known in town for delivering only quality furniture. His staff were skilled and although he expected a lot from his employees, he paid them well.

A few minutes after the embarrassing episode, Bigotes came to our usual workbench, and I greeted him, like always. He looked angry and ashamed. I asked if he had any chairs for me to carve. That simple question was all it took to set him off. "Why am I teaching you everything I know? I know you are learning so you can take my job! I am a fool, showing you all this. Tomorrow, you will stab me in the back, and Romero will throw me out on the street!" he raged, discharging all his anger and frustration on me. His anger was a lot stronger than his drunken breath.

I couldn't believe he considered me a threat. Getting him fired was the last thing I wanted. He was my mentor in the art of woodcarving, and I looked up to him despite the untreated alcohol addiction that was interfering with his work. He was angry for being publicly humiliated, and now, he was feeling ashamed in front of his pupil, resentful and powerless. I knew he was angry at Mr. Romero for shaming him and at the system that left him feeling oppressed and powerless, but even so, I was shocked by the rage driving his reaction. For a crazy moment, I imagined carving chisels flying at me. Quitting was out of the question for him in the current collapsed economy, however, so he just had to suck it up and take the abuse without complaint. What hurt me was the fact that I could not tell him the real reason I was learning to carve wood. I hadn't shared my plan to "disappear" from Peru in a few months with anyone at the factory because so many people were being denied visas every day, and I didn't want them to think I was crazy. Instead, I just took my set of carving chisels, grabbed my jacket, and never looked back.

Losing my job was a minor setback, but my determination to emigrate continued strong. I needed to start earning money to cover the passport prerequisite costs and fees. My father had been working two jobs and my mother had become a door-to-door salesperson to help make ends meet. The small convenience store had shut down because we didn't have enough money to restock it with essential food items. As a peddler, my mother sold T-shirts, underwear, and towels in different neighborhoods, carrying two heavy boxes filled with merchandise for miles every day. I remember having heartfelt conversations about the deteriorating family finances with my mom. "We will make it through this, together son" she said. I asked my mom to give me two boxes of the merchandise so I could sell it in another town to help my family and begin saving money.

I invited my friend Angel to join me in selling on the streets and on villages outside the city. We unraveled the secrets of each village's rhythms and found out the days when the villagers got paid for delivering milk or selling the farmers' crops. Those were the times when people had money to spend. At dawn, Angel and I set out with our two heavy boxes filled with treasures, ready to sell them all. With determination, we walked along the cobblestone paths in the village. Like modern troubadours, we visited each home, sharing stories about our goods and hoping to connect with the locals while bringing news from the city.

After a few days, we rented a tricycle to transport our boxes, making our journeys smoother and more enjoyable. With the tricycle, our sales increased, and we happily pedaled from farm to farm, taking turns. There were scary moments when angry dogs chased us, spurring one of us to pedal furiously while the other hurled rocks to keep them at bay. But this added a bit of excitement to our informal business venture. Understandably, a few customers didn't have cash on hand, so they paid us with guinea pigs, hens, or bags of fruit.

Some days were profitable, while others left us worn out and empty handed. I discovered that success in sales depended on persistence. Reading Og Mandino's widely popular book, *The World's Greatest Salesman,* kept me motivated. Mandino emphasized the law of averages—the more sales calls you make, the higher the likelihood of making a sale. I applied this principle and found it effective.

As my 18th birthday neared, I was pleased that my plans to migrate were progressing. I even managed to assist my siblings in acquiring their school supplies and still save some money for the passport application. Yet, the approach of my 18th birthday was bittersweet, for I knew it would be my final festivity on Peruvian soil. My mind kept wandering to the unhappy awareness that my closest friends would soon fade from my daily life. As if that weren't enough, this birthday carried another unexpected weight, as it marked the grim anniversary of what we sarcastically called "the great robbery." Exactly a year ago, on my 17th birthday, under the veil of night between 2 and 4 am, our home was robbed by two adults and a child. They had cut the metal bars guarding the window facing the street, creating a hole just big enough for a 10-year-old to slither through. While we slept peacefully, they had quietly stolen our TV, our cherished record player, a trove of LP music albums, and most of the pots, pans, dishes, glasses, and appliances in our kitchen. My entire family had grappled with shock and indignation when morning revealed the wreckage. After reporting the robbery to the police, we spent the day shrouded in disbelief. With all the worry and chaos, my birthday had slipped by unnoticed, overshadowed by a sense of sadness and helplessness that lingered in my family's memories for years.

Caught in the tapestry of poignant memories and my own swirling emotions around my upcoming departure, I opted to forego any celebration for my 18th birthday. When the fateful day arrived, the scent of freshly baked apple cake wafted through the air, a comforting aroma of familial warmth. My mom had something to do with that caring surprise. We assembled around the table in front of the delicious cake, with a single candle in its center. As the flame flickered to life, my family serenaded me with the familiar strains of "Happy Birthday." It was a quiet affair, but in the simplicity of that moment, there was a depth of connection that transcended the need for grandiosity.

A few weeks after my birthday, my long-awaited passport finally arrived, triggering a flurry of activity over the next few days, as I scrambled to assemble the remaining documents for the next step: A pilgrimage to the U.S. Embassy in the heart of Lima. I kept my secret like a clandestine treasure; only my dearest kin were privy to my plan to seek a U.S. visa in Lima. The prospect of journeying to the sprawling metropolis was daunting — my inaugural solo expedition. In 1986, Lima was home to a staggering one-quarter of Peru's total population of approximately 25 million. It's no exaggeration when I say that the enormity of the cityscape loomed large. Yet, fear found solace in the knowledge that I had a tiny haven of safety awaiting me. My Aunt Pocha, who lived in Lima, had graciously extended the sanctuary of her home to help me pursue the holy grail of securing a tourist visa.

Tourist Visa: The Big Gamble

The 16-hour bus ride to Lima was exhausting. The only interstate highway that connected Arequipa to Lima was the Pan American Highway. It was the same highway my dad had traveled countless times when he had served in the Peruvian Air Force 25 years earlier. Constructed in the mid-1930s, the Pan American Highway linked numerous countries across the Western hemisphere, stretching from Alaska to Argentina. The Peruvian section of the highway had suffered from considerable neglect, however, reflecting the country's economic decline. As I traveled to Lima, I encountered a road riddled with potholes—some patched but many wide open. Back then, bus drivers needed additional skills that drivers in developed countries don't typically need. They had to stay on their toes at all times, navigating all the potholes and maneuvering the bus with finesse to prevent accidents, all while blasting loud music from the cassette player. Along the way, we saw numerous broken-down buses, seemingly driven by less-skilled drivers, stranded on the roadside with damaged suspension systems.

The most frightening thing about the trip was not the decaying road. It was the fear of being assaulted and robbed by highway criminals, kidnappers, or Shining Path guerrillas. Sometimes when buses passed through *zonas controladas,* or areas controlled by Shining Path guerrillas, they would be intercepted and a "guerrilla tax" would be demanded from all passengers, who would also be forced to accept propaganda materials.

Fortunately, our journey had only one major hiccup. It happened near the famous Nazca Lines—ancient drawings etched into the Earth, visible only from high above. About a year earlier, a mudslide had blocked the paved road, forcing cars to detour through a sandy desert area. There was a notorious spot on this detour where most vehicles got stuck, including our bus. It was a huge hole filled with sand, and it trapped us around midnight. To free ourselves, all of us passengers had to pitch in. We worked together for hours, gathering rocks to construct a makeshift ramp that would give the tires some level of traction. Once the ramp was ready, all

40 of us worked as a team to push the bus out of the hole. In no time, we were back on track, continuing our journey. Finally, we arrived in Lima safely, with no further incidents or harassment by criminals.

Once we arrived, I shifted into what I thought of as "Lima mode." That is, pretending to be calm and confident when I was actually hyperalert, aware of every detail of my surroundings. Being in Lima mode meant taking smart precautions to minimize the chances of being robbed. I was careful to spread the cash I was carrying among as many different pockets as I could, even stashing some in my socks. I also tried to talk faster and to speak with the *Criollo* accent that was unique to Lima natives. I avoided acting humble or uncertain, hoping that if I hid my identity and managed to fit in, people would assume I was from Lima, and I would be less vulnerable.

Aunt Pocha lived in a neighborhood known for its high crime rates. She ran a *pensión*, offering working-class folks affordable and satisfying meals. Like many others, Aunt Pocha had migrated to Lima from the Valley of Volcanoes two decades ago. She was warm and caring but also business-savvy. She wasted no time in explaining the house rules and the meal prices. I knew that she had to be well-organized to survive the challenges of living in Lima, and I was just grateful that she welcomed me into her home for four days and allowed me to spend time with my cousins.

The day after I arrived in Lima was my big day at the U.S. Embassy. Early that morning, I stared in the mirror, admiring myself in my very first business suit, which my dad and I had purchased a week earlier. I held a folder with all the documentation for the interview. The folder contained the visa request forms; my parents' list of assets, property taxes, and bank statements; affidavits of support; my passport; and my school reports...I was ready. *Ricardo*, I said to myself in the mirror, *the journey to the United States of America starts with a visa, and a visa is what I will receive today!* I left the room feeling confident and ready to conquer the world. I kissed Aunt Po-cha goodbye and left the house to grab a taxi to the Embassy in full Lima mode.

The taxi dropped me off a couple of blocks away from the Embassy in Lima's affluent Miraflores District. "We can't get any closer," the driver said, "the roads are blocked." The Embassy was surrounded by cement barricades that had been erected after it had been reported that the Shining Path planned to target American-owned or sponsored organizations. "Thank you, sir," I said to the driver, as I paid for the ride and got out of the cab. I walked down the street and weaved through the crowd of mostly young and middle-aged people, all of whom looked either busy or confused like me. The noise got louder as I got closer to the Embassy. Everyone looked tense, each in his or her own world. Street sellers of all trades loudly advertised their snacks, ice cream, and services. The ones with typewriters perched on their laps offered to type applicants' official visa request forms; others had cameras for taking passport photos; and more than a few tiny offices advertised photocopy services.

I finally found the line for visa applicants. "Oh, what luck!" I said out loud, "the line is near the entrance!" A middle-aged man in front of me laughed. "Look, son," he corrected me, "the line loops around the entire block!" My heart sank as I lifted my chin and looked around. He was right, the line was incredibly long and it was only 8:30 am. "A lot of folks get in line at 4 am," the man said. "Most of the early birds are applicants, but some are people who make a living by 'reserving spots' in the line, which they then sell to rich people who come at 8:30 am, right when the Embassy opens its doors to the public." Listening to his words, I knew I was going to be there all day.

It took many hours, but I finally made it inside. I joined the tense, quiet environment in the crowded waiting room. I silently started reciting the Lord's Prayer, and then, when I was about to start the Hail Mary, I paused and looked around. That was when I noticed that I wasn't the only one praying for a U.S. visa. Honestly, immigration waiting rooms should be declared *houses of prayer*. Most of the people there were consciously attempting to connect with a higher power while waiting their turn. They were silently praying, wishing, asking for, and even demanding a perfect, successful interview. God is "loved" there like never before. People were praying with an intensity and a level of devotion that most priests can only dream of at their churches on Sunday mornings. Except that instead of bibles, the people in these *houses of prayer* held onto their immigration folders and manila envelopes as if they contained the original holy scriptures.

"Ricardo Sánchez, window number four," I heard, abruptly interrupting my own prayer. I quickly stood up and brought my attention back to the present as I walked toward window number four. A middle-age, partially bald white man was waiting for me on the other side of the window. His metal name tag read: Mr. Rigby-Smith.

"Good morning, sir, I am here to apply for a tourist visa," I said. "Did you bring all the required documents?" He asked. "Yes, sir," I said, "they are all right here in the folder."

He looked at my face and asked, "How old are you?" "I just turned 18, sir," I said. "Let me see, are you Samuel?" He asked. "No, sir, I am Ricardo," I said. "Look, you are an adult according to Peruvian law," he said. "Unless you are a minor, all documents must be in your name—bank accounts, assets, property taxes, and so forth," he added. For a moment, I thought he was joking. I even smiled and said to myself, *that's a good joke.* He didn't smile back. As if reading my thoughts, he said, "I am not joking. That is exactly what is required if you want to apply for a visa." I stared at his eyes for five long seconds and saw not a trace of humor on his face. I nodded in total confusion, looked down, and stepped away from the window.

As I walked away, disconcerted, I thought of all the efforts and sacrifices my family and I had made to get me to this point. *The entire visa process was so unfair—months and months of preparation, all for nothing,* I thought. I realized how the system was rigged. *Visas were designed for rich people who could easily assign assets and bank accounts to their relatives' names,* I thought. *How else could someone my age ever get a visa?*

I left the Embassy in denial. My dreams and the future I had been building had suffered a huge blow, and everything was going to pieces. I wanted to scream to the four winds and let out all the sadness and anger inside me. I walked a few blocks to a park bench facing the Pacific Ocean, where I sat down and cried. I felt the ocean in my eyes and a crater in my heart. *"¿Qué será de mi?"* ("What will become of me?") I asked over and over again. My heart was bleeding, and I didn't know how to repair it. More than anything, I felt shame at the thought of returning home as a total failure, a laughingstock.

There I was in Lima, just like my father, who had eagerly tried to chase the American Dream 25 years ago. We both had known it wasn't going to be easy. His rite of passage was almost risking his life in Vietnam, while my passage had just been totally blocked. *With so much injustice everywhere, no wonder so many people become rebels*, I thought. *Dreams do not come true in Peru unless you are well-connected or have the recommendation of someone with influence.* It was not just the visa process, it was also about who gets education, health services, food, and jobs. *Who controls Peru, the Western Hemisphere, the world?* I was beyond frustrated.

I spent the entire bus ride back to Arequipa thinking about the unjust world we lived in. I was feeling so disappointed and depressed that if the bus had been kidnapped, I wouldn't have even cared. I cried out of impotence; and I saw Mr. Bigotes in my mind's eye and imagined how he must have felt the day I left my job—like a powerless peasant who couldn't say or do anything. I thought of my younger siblings and their future.

My parents were happy to see me but sad about the outcome at the Embassy. The weeks that followed brought back those dreadful Sunday afternoons. This time, I just didn't want to wake up. The pain from the "high" and fallout from the visa fiasco felt like it would drown me. I was on my way to becoming a burden to my family instead of a contributor. I had aspired to be their hope and savior, but I had failed miserably.

The love and support of my family helped get me through the next few dark days, and gradually, I began to feel hope again. I began to wear my purple D.C. t-shirt again, too. The more strength I gained, the louder the same message echoed within my soul, *you must go to America!* I had many tense conversations with my parents, verbally exploring every crazy scenario. I even asked my parents to put our house, the family bank account, and my dad's 1964 rusty Chevy taxi in my name (of course, they said, "No!"). Another scenario I came up with was borrowing money from relatives to create a bank account in my name so I could reapply for a visa. But all those scenarios were crazy and absurd—none of my relatives had large sums of money, and even if they did, they would never have lent it to a naïve 18-year-old like me. Nevertheless, America was on my mind constantly. I daydreamed about my life there every day; it was as if my soul was already in Washington, D.C.

A week after I had returned to Arequipa, I was back selling clothing in nearby villages with Angel. One day, on one of our long walks between farms, we stumbled onto a small creek. Our backpacks and boxes were filled with merchandise, but we needed to cross to the other side to reach our destination. Suddenly, another crazy thought struck me: "What if I cross the river?" I said aloud. Angel turned around and laughed. "What river? This is a creek! Where's the river exactly? I know we're tired and hungry, but you've gone over the edge, my man!" I had been thinking about the Rio Grande, of course, but Angel had no idea what I was talking about and I certainly wasn't going to tell him. I quickly corrected myself and said, "Of course, I meant to say 'creek,' not 'river.'"

We crossed the creek and went on with our business, but my mind was thinking nonstop about my new plan. I'd heard stories of people crossing the Rio Grande. I knew how to swim. Plus, I was 18, and some kids became soldiers at 18. *I can do this*, I thought.

That night, I talked to my parents about my latest "aha" moment. They rolled their eyes, and I could see them thinking, *Oh no, here we go again!* If there had been an award for being the biggest pain in the ass to one's parents, I would have won it, hands down. "That's crazy!" my parents said. "How are you going to get to the border? We have heard horrible stories of people being robbed, assaulted, and even killed! Besides, we don't know anyone who could help with stuff like that." They gave me reason after reason, trying to talk me out of this latest crazy idea. Finally, I asked, "What if Aunt Pocha knows somebody in Lima who could help? Can we call her, Papa?" He refused to call at first, and for several weeks, he kept making excuses not to call. But one day, I caught him off guard while he was relaxing at home, and he finally agreed to make the call with me at his side.

The usual greetings and inquiries about each and every family member that precede every Peruvian phone call seemed never-ending that day. I noticed my dad trying to stall so he wouldn't have to get to the point of the conversation, but the pressure he felt over the cost of the long-distance call forced his hand. Finally, he asked, "Do you happen to know anybody in Lima who might be able to help someone get into Mexico and cross the U.S. border?" Aunt Pocha paused. Then, she said, "I know a family whose son has emigrated. I think he crossed the border a few months ago. I can ask his relatives if they know anyone. If so, I'll get back to you." I was glued to the back of the phone that my dad was holding, and my hopes soared as I listened to this exchange.

A week later, Aunt Pocha called back and gave us the information that we needed. "I contacted that family and they say there is a 'travel agency' that helps people with the border-crossing process," she said. "They charge $3,000 in total," she said, adding that half the money must be paid prior to the trip, and the other half would be due within six months of crossing. "If you are able to raise the money in two months, there is a group that is traveling around Christmas time." My dad froze. "We will discuss it here, and I will call you back in the next few days," he finally said.

After he had hung up, my dad said, "It costs too much money. There is no way we can afford it. How are we going to raise $1,500?" My dad felt terribly bad that Aunt Pocha had to be involved. I, too, felt bad. I was talking my parents and relatives into risking all they had—family relationships, assets, and trust. I had no words to express how bad I was feeling, asking for money while knowing the struggles we were having at home. I left the room, wanting to be alone. My head was spinning after the phone call, as I tried to process what Aunt Pocha had said and reconcile what I knew I needed to do with what I now knew it would cost.

Despite their initial objections, my parents knew by now how determined I was to go to America, and somehow, they knew I would not let that aspiration go. My parents had $95 saved in the bank. Obviously, that wasn't going to cut it, so our next step was to begin asking our relatives to lend me some money. Over the next few days, my dad and I visited several relatives who had stable jobs, and we collected $300, which I promised to repay as soon as I could. Mr. Romero offered to lend me $700, but because his offer included paying 150% in annual interest, we respectfully declined.

Inflation was so high, and the economy was spiraling downward so quickly that 150% was actually quite reasonable at the time, but it was more than I could commit to repaying. Eventually, my dad ended up borrowing $1,200 from a bank, using our house as collateral. At this point, we knew there was no turning back.

Aunt Pocha signed a contract on our behalf with the "travel agency." By signing, she was agreeing to be a guarantor to pay the remaining $1,500 within six months of my arrival in the U.S. Like my dad, she also had to use her house (which included her *pensión* business) as collateral. The weight of this heavy responsibility made me realize that I was not a kid anymore. If I failed, both my family and my aunt's family could end up homeless. I already felt crushed by the weight of those debts, and not only hadn't I even left yet, but it was only October—there were still two months to go!

November came and I switched from selling clothes to selling toys and Nativity scenes, still door to door, complete with miniature clay figures of Joseph, Mother Mary, and baby Jesus, as well as the camels, horses, and cows in the barn. The boxes were twice as heavy as before, and Angel and I changed our sales pitch, as well. "Would you like to bring peace, joy, and prosperity home this Christmas season? Bring in the spirit of baby Jesus by allowing the entire holy family to enter your home today. Each Nativity set has been blessed with holy water, and baby Jesus will personally bless your home and family!"

For the families who couldn't afford to pay for an entire new set, we offered the merchandise that had been chipped or damaged somewhere along the way at a much lower price. As we sold more and more Nativity sets and I gained more confidence, I found myself expanding my creativity to generate additional sales. For me, the Christmas season of 1986 meant prosperity not only in terms of sales, but also because of the feelings of becoming self-sufficient, experiencing the fruits of persistence, and dreaming big again.

Knowing that this would be my last Christmas in Peru, however, I silently began to grieve the loss of significant relationships once again. I became nicer, wanting to cherish each relationship in the short time I had left before it was time to travel. A week later, news came from Lima that my group's departure had been rescheduled for January, but I was still required to go to Lima for a "travel training workshop" at the agency. During the 5-day workshop, an instructor walked me and the rest of the group through the entire process. We learned about the routes we would take, the risks, how to handle unexpected situations, and many other details. We also learned a lot about Mexico—everything from the currency to famous people, the national anthem, and the names of the current and former presidents. We even had to practice speaking Spanish with a Mexican accent and learn basic information about various places in Mexico. The staff said that we needed to know all these things in case we were caught somewhere along the journey. If the authorities thought we were Mexican, they explained, they would only deport us to Mexico instead of sending us all the way back to Peru. The owner of the travel agency appeared periodically to check on our progress. He seemed to be on top of things—the type of person who inspired confidence. After the training ended, I returned to Arequipa to celebrate my last Christmas and New Year's with my family and friends.

Goodbye For Now or Forever?

On a cloudy afternoon in January 1987, a week into the new year, my parents and siblings gathered around the table to say goodbye to me. We all hugged, said how much we loved each other, and cried together. I felt the full extent of my mother's pain when she said, "may God take care of you, my son, for I don't know if I will ever see you again." My heart ached even worse when I saw my baby siblings, holding hands next to my mom with tears in their eyes, as if saying "please, don't leave us."

As we stepped out of the house, my dad insisted we capture this moment to preserve the memory. I knew he was thinking that it might be the last time we would ever be all together. We didn't own a camera, so we hurried to the local photographer on our way to the bus terminal. Arriving at the studio, the photographer told us to smile for the camera, but try as we might, none of us could muster a smile. The photo wasn't about smiles or happiness. On that day, it was sadness and tears that bonded us, and that was alright.

As the bus pulled away from my hometown, tears streamed down my face and my heart felt weighed down by everything and everyone I was leaving behind. Overwhelmed with emotion, I closed my eyes, hoping sleep would ease the pain. It felt like the world I knew was slipping away, perhaps forever.

After I got to Lima, I stayed at Aunt Pocha's place for a few days, waiting for my group's departure date. On the big day, I said goodbye to Aunt Pocha and my cousins before heading to the airport. Aunt Pocha couldn't come with me because she had to cook for her clients and take care of the house. "God bless you, Ricardo, I hope you achieve all your dreams," she said before I left in a taxi for Jorge Chavez International Airport.

At the airport, I spotted fellow members of our group, all standing with their families. They seemed composed, following the instructions from our training workshop. According to the plan, if questioned about our destination, we were to say we were taking a short vacation in Acapulco, Mexico, and returning to Peru in four days. We had been told to travel light, with just a carry-on, and to dress in business casual attire. Also, we were to avoid interactions or eye contact with others in the group in airports or bus terminals.

As I neared the check-in line, a wave of emotion washed over me. The quiet anguish of people bidding farewell to their family members and loved ones pierced my heart. It felt like a poignant dance of goodbyes, each step laden with unspoken sorrow. How much harder it must have been to part ways with a forced smile, a gentle hug, or a simple handshake. Yet, no one would shed tears at the airport over a mere four-day separation. To do so would risk exposing the delicate web of secrets, potentially endangering both themselves and those left behind. After all, we had been warned about widespread corruption among immigration and law enforcement authorities. Law enforcement officers sometimes stopped travelers in the airport hallways or at the gates, looking for slip-ups and using any excuse to demand bribes. That's why it was so important to avoid heartfelt farewells.

We checked in separately, pretending not to know each other, passed through the immigration checkpoint, and went into the international flights section. Spreading out, we waited at the gate, occasionally glancing at each other out of the corner of our eyes, until it was time to board the plane. As I stepped onto the aircraft, a wave of relief washed over me, knowing we were beyond the reach of immigration's scrutiny. Yet, behind my calm exterior, a storm of emotions brewed within. Excitement tingled through my veins because it was my first time ever in an airplane, yet my heart was also heavy with sorrow as I thought about my loved ones. As the plane ascended, my gaze drifted to the vast expanse below. Peru's landscape unfurled beneath me. Gazing out the window, it wasn't merely separation from family that gripped me, but a profound sense of disconnection from the land, the very essence of my heritage. In that moment, I grappled with an unsettling sense of cultural dissonance, as if my identity were being pulled apart at its seams.

If I had had a tourist visa to the U.S. and knew I could travel back to Peru, I would have been a hundred times less anxious, I suppose. However, emigrating one-way with the risk of maybe never arriving at my destination and no idea when or if I would ever be able to return, put me in a sort of purgatory state—neither in heaven nor in hell. I wondered how other immigrants throughout history must have felt when they left their homes to migrate to other lands. I thought of the Irish, Italians, and Germans, many of whom left to escape poverty, and the Africans, who were brought against their will and forced to leave their ancestral lands to live in faraway lands. My empathy for migrants and refugees all over the world was suddenly huge.

During our connecting flight in Panama, an incident in Immigration and Customs put us all on edge. A member of our group was questioned, causing a hold-up in the line. Our guide, swift and discreet, cut through the line and intervened.

Intrigued, I craned my neck to catch a glimpse of what was happening. The guide quietly exchanged a few words with the officer, handed over his passport, and after a mysterious exchange, the line surged forward like magic. We knew what had just happened, but we couldn't talk about it. We were "total strangers."

Mexican Visa to Guatemala?

We had been warned to be flexible and trust the guides. Because the nature of the trip, we had no say about the logistics or sudden changes in plans. We had been told that our next flight would be to Mexico, but right before boarding the next flight in Panama, we were told that we were going to Guatemala, instead. By 1987, so many Peruvians were fleeing the country that many Latin American countries had begun instituting quotas for Peruvian travelers. Mexico was one of the countries that now had strict visa limits for Peruvians, especially young people. The new plan was to get ourselves mentally ready to take the same routes that many Central Americans had to take to reach the U.S. border.

Once we got to Guatemala City, our air travels were over. From there, we journeyed by bus and on foot toward the Guatemala-Mexico border and crossed into Southern Mexico, continuing our month-long journey North. We walked for miles, crossed five rivers, and rode on the backs of pickup trucks and buses along highways and dirt roads, crossing around 2,000 miles of Mexico by land. Many buses were stopped at random by the Mexican police, known as the *Federales,* at highway inspection points. The *Federales* were famous for their ability to detect non-Mexicans trying to get to the Mexico-U.S. border. At first, I wondered, how do they know so much about people, seemingly catching their scent from miles away? Later, I realized that it was simple; they were so strongly motivated by greed that they would do anything for a bribe. People feared them not because they represented the law, but because they were often involved in shady dealings themselves. In all, we were stopped five times for highway inspections. Each time, all suspected non-Mexicans were removed from the bus, forced to walk to the back side, and asked to pay a bribe. After we paid, the "law enforcement officers" allowed us to reboard to continue the ride. The routine became so normal that once, I even waved goodbye to one of the officers from the bus window. The officer smiled and waved back at me as the bus departed.

On one of the inspections at a small-town bus terminal, the *Federales* were not like the rest. The inspection started out just like the others. The officers stopped the bus, boarded, and slowly walked toward the back, scrutinizing everyone aboard while asking questions and using their well-honed skills to identify the non-Mexicans. Seven people were picked—two Salvadorans, three Guatemalans, and two Peruvians—a guy named Freddy and me. I don't know what possessed the officers that day, but they were extremely angry, and they treated us like dangerous criminals. Instead of walking us off the bus like usual, they used physical force to pull us off the bus, punching and kicking us. Once we were off the bus, they ordered us at gunpoint to put our hands behind our heads while cursing, yelling, and threatening to kill us if we tried to run away. One of the officers pushed Freddy from behind, and Freddy made the mistake of tightening his body, as if resisting. The officer interpreted his automatic reflex as an act of defiance and punched Freddy in the face, kicking him in the stomach as he fell to the ground. I tried to help him stand up, but another officer pushed me hard and said, "Don't move, mother fucker, or I'll blow your brains out!" pointing his gun at my face.

The *Federales* ordered the bus driver to leave the terminal without us because we were going to be arrested and sent to jail. The officers made us line up and put our hands on the shoulders of the person in front of us. Then, they made us walk half a block towards the cruiser. By this time, curious pedestrians had gathered in the street to see what was happening. The *Federales* continued their show of arresting us like a band of criminals, probably trying to show everyone in the community how tough they were against the outlaws. Once we were sardined in the police cruiser, the officers ended their show. They drove a few blocks and then stopped and demanded bribes. After they collected a few hundred dollars from us, they put on their police sirens and flashing lights and sped off with us still in the back of the car, as if they were chasing another band of criminals. This time, they were speeding to catch our bus. Fortunately, several miles away from the town, we caught up with the bus. The driver stopped and allowed us to continue our journey North as if nothing had happened.

Our small group of Peruvians managed to regroup again at a bus terminal in Tijuana to prepare for the taxi ride to the next hotel. Of course, we made sure to maintain some distance from each other at the terminal, as we'd been trained, but we still exchanged subtle glances from time to time. When we stepped outside and into the parking lot, we split into small groups of three or four and got into taxis, almost like little family units.

Once we were in our assigned taxicab, the three of us in my group relaxed and started to talk normally. But that turned out to be a big mistake. Our driver was not just a random person, as we'd assumed. Not five minutes out of the bus terminal, the driver pulled over behind a police patrol car and stopped. "Son of a bitch!" said my companion who was sitting in the front seat. "What do you think you are doing?!" we angrily asked the driver. The driver quickly jumped out of the car before we had a chance to react.

Next thing we knew, two *Federales* were standing on either side of the taxi, insisting that we show them our "Certified International Tourist Identification" documents. These documents didn't exist, of course, they had made them up to increase their chances of getting bribes from us. We showed them our valid passports, but these obviously didn't satisfy their demands. The police used our alleged lack of documentation as an excuse to arrest us. At gun point, they demanded we exit the taxi and board the police cruiser, and we were forced to squeeze into the back seat, along with our backpacks or carry-ons. As we headed toward the police station, they threatened to deport us for not having the made-up documents unless we each gave them $700.

Initially, their threats rattled us, but my street-smart companions, experienced in dealing with corrupt officers and robbers in the streets of Lima, quickly saw through their bluff. I also tried to act tough, going into "Lima mode." My companions, who were a few years older than me, boldly told the officers, "Ok, go ahead and take us to the police station and deport us if you want. We don't care. In fact, why don't you take all our possessions while you're at it! But the moment we get back, we will report you to your superiors and call the Peruvian consulate. So, go ahead and do whatever you want, man." The police did not expect non-compliance; they shouted at us and doubled down on their threats to deport us. We knew we were taking a huge risk. After all, we were going up against armed officers with the authority of the law. For a moment, I thought they might drive us to a dark alley and beat us up. After a few minutes of riding—and loudly arguing—the cruiser stopped in front of the police station. Maybe the officers thought that seeing the station would make us yield to their assault. We sat there for a few moments in tense silence; time was ticking for them and for us. The longer they retained us in the cruiser in front of the police station parking lot, the more suspicious they looked to their supervisors, who worked in the building. Time was on our side, and the combination of panic and fear we were feeling somehow sustained our courage.

"*Hijos de su chingada madre!*" ("sons of bitches!") said the angry officer in the driver's seat, "Give us $300 each, and get the fuck out of the car!" "We don't have that kind of money," we replied. "How can we give you what we don't have, officer?" It was strange that these corrupt officers didn't seem to realize that most people arrive at the border with little to no cash. If we had money, wouldn't we have found a way to get a tourist visa and fly directly to the U.S.?

The officers pulled out their guns again and pointed them at us, swearing and cursing in Mexican slang as they growled, "Give us all you have in your wallets and pockets, all of it!" They forced us take off our shoes and socks and they collected all the money from our backpacks and carry-ons. In total, their assault in the police station parking lot netted them $107.50. A long 10-second silence followed our flurry of activity in the cramped backseat of the squad car. It wasn't a lot, but we truly had given them everything we had. We still feared for our lives, not knowing how this was going to end. What if they shot us and dumped us in the river? What if they detained and deported us anyway? What if they took all our belongings and left us naked in the street? I didn't know what to think anymore.

Somehow, the silence seemed to bring out the officer's guilt or 'human side'—I'm not sure which—and they surprised us by giving us back $7.50. "Take the change," they said, "you will need it for your tacos and to reach your hotel tonight." They drove us a few blocks away and dumped us in an ally in the middle of a Tijuana ghetto.

Still reeling from the encounter in the dark alley, the three of us remained on high alert, desperate to find our way to the designated hotel. Emerging from the shadows onto a nearby sidewalk, we stumbled upon a street food vendor— an elderly woman selling tacos from a makeshift stall. Despite our hunger, we refrained from eating, eager to escape the streets of Tijuana as quickly as possible. From that moment on, our trust in strangers evaporated, and every passing shadow seemed to conceal a potential threat. We walked separately but in the same direction, attempting to blend in with the locals despite our obvious foreign appearance. After walking seven miles, we arrived at the hotel around midnight, only to discover that half of our group was missing, including the guide. In the lobby, we waited anxiously, adhering to the instructions given the day before. After three tense hours, the guide finally arrived with four other group members, bringing a sense of relief amidst the uncertainty. However, there was still no sign of the last two missing group members—Rosita and her son Pedro.

We checked in and headed to our rooms. As usual, we were reminded not to interact with anyone or open the door, not even for the cleaning crew. We were not allowed to open the curtains or peek through the windows, either. Our guides would bring sandwiches, we were told, and we shouldn't do anything until the guides came to give us instructions for the next move. If anyone knocked, we were to say a code word and we should only open the door if the person who had knocked replied with a matching code word.

As time went on, I came to understand the grim truth: Our guides weren't just shielding us from corrupt *Federales*; they were also fending off the looming threat of abduction by other guides from rival "agencies." It was a chilling realization that each of us was seen as a commodity with a price tag, mere merchandise that hadn't yet been fully paid for. This realization wasn't just deeply unsettling, it shook me to my core. It meant that we, like millions of other immigrants, were just unwitting pawns in a sprawling human trafficking network.

In Tijuana, a "guide" morphs into a "coyote" as one gets close to the border. A guide serves as an orchestrator of logistics, a guardian of schedules, and a paragon of composure in the face of adversity. He is the refined maestro of the journey, navigating complexities with finesse and precision. A coyote, on the other hand, is wild, serving just one purpose—to facilitate the passage across the treacherous terrain known as the Mexico-U.S. border. Coyotes must navigate hazards using their intimate knowledge of the land. They are the unsung heroes of clandestine crossings, tackling the most perilous and grueling tasks with unwavering resolve. While both guides and coyotes face the constant specter of capture and detention by law enforcement, coyotes traverse the terrain with an unparalleled audacity, mastering darkness as adeptly as light. In the surreptitious world of border crossings, they reign supreme as the captains of clandestine voyages, wielding absolute authority and power. At the border's edge, they are both essential and enigmatic, occupying a paradoxical space as a necessary evil in the pursuit of successful migration.

As I reflected upon these contrasting personas, someone suddenly started pounding on the door. Knock, knock, knock!! My companions quickly stopped whispering, and total silence filled the room. "Open the door!" someone said from the hallway. We remained silent. Knock, knock, knock!! "Open the door!" The person said again, more insistently. We kept waiting for the code word, but the person didn't say it. "Open the door! God damn it!" the man yelled. We peeked through the door peephole and saw a different guide. But he was with Rosita and her son! So, we said one word, "*Chavo?*" He responded, "*Kiko.*" We threw open the door. The guide was supposed to say the code word at the beginning, but I guess he didn't get the memo.

Once we shut the door, Rosita immediately burst into tears. We asked what had happened, but she was crying so hard that she couldn't speak. Her son Pedro looked confused; he seemed to be in shock as he slumped down in one corner of the room. Rosita looked exhausted, nauseated, and disgusted. It was obvious that she was in physical and psychological pain. Without saying a word, she ran to the bathroom, and through the door, we could hear her crying even more.

When she finally emerged, it was clear from her demeanor and emotional state that she had been badly abused. Although she wanted to hide it, she finally shared what had happened. She and her son had taken a taxicab from the airport like the rest of the group, and the taxi driver turned them in to a couple of corrupt police officers, just like ours had done. Not happy with the bribe money they managed to get from her, the officers took Rosita and her son to an empty construction site, where they raped Rosita in front of her child. After that, the police officers drove around for a while before leaving them on the street, far from their destination. In shock and desperation, Rosita and her son walked for hours before they managed to find the hotel, where they met the new guide, who was waiting for them in the hotel lobby.

We didn't know what to say, but we were all filled with anger, fear, impotence, and hatred towards the people who had committed this horrendous act. Things like this were not supposed to happen to elementary schoolteachers like Rosita or her young son, who would have to carry this trauma for the rest of his life. After hearing what had happened, the guide did not say much except that he was ashamed that his countrymen had committed such a horrendous act.

As we tried to figure out how to comfort someone in such obvious emotional distress, we were abruptly interrupted by our guide, who briskly reminded us of the need to adhere to the day's itinerary. He instructed everyone to be prepared to depart from the hotel at 7:00 pm. "We'll take public transportation to another place on the outskirts of the city, close to the border. Tonight, we cross," he said. He left a few bags of sandwiches for us on the bed and exited the room. The men in the room decided to sleep on the floor while Rosita and Pedro napped in the beds. We all were cognizant that we needed to rest so we'd be ready for what was ahead of us that night.

The Spirit of Rambo

Around 7:00 pm, the guide escorted us to a nearby bus stop to catch the bus to the northern outskirts of the city. The bus drove through dozens of neighborhoods as we passed busy business districts, poor shantytowns, and then, dusty, unpaved roads with few or no streetlights. When the bus reached the end of its route, the driver looked in his rearview mirror and called out loudly, "This is the end, everyone has to get off."

We were scattered throughout the bus, pretending we didn't know each other. We got off the bus quietly and made our way through the dimly lit, unpaved streets of the shantytown. Street dogs trailed behind us, barking and poised to pounce. Remembering a childhood trick, we picked up rocks from the ground and threw a few, causing the dogs to halt their pursuit. The area looked as if it had been informally populated a year or two before. Some houses had walls made of piles of stones with tarps or cheap corrugated metal sheets as roofs. Some had electricity, others did not. They were the homes of marginalized and impoverished but resilient people.

Our "tour" of the neighborhood came to an end when we entered one of those humble homes. Much to our surprise, the living room was packed with Central Americans and Mexicans. Some were sitting on the floor, while others stood in the crowed space. There were 33 people in total. Some of the children looked to be about 10 years old. Most were with at least one parent. A teenager was there with an older relative, maybe a grandparent, who was maybe in his 60s. There were also a few unaccompanied minors and some older teenagers like me.

Upon seeing the large crowd, the looks on the faces of my fellow Peruvians mirrored my own. We were all thinking the same thing, *What the hell? Nobody had told us anything about joining a big group of strangers!* Although most people in the room looked exhausted, we couldn't help but stay in *trust no one* mode. Some people were talking to each other; others were catching up on hours or days of missed sleep. We just stood there until a Mexican lady came over and offered us some tacos. She spoke to us in a compassionate tone and said, "Please eat as much as you can. God only knows when your next meal will be."

At the center of the living room, there was a big pile of clothes and backpacks. That was where we would have to leave all our belongings—our backpacks, shoes, and suits. We were not supposed to bring anything with us. I knew I'd have to part with my brand-new business suit and backpack soon, but I hesitated. I'd worked hard to buy that suit, and I'd only worn it twice.

Suddenly, an authoritative voice rose above the noise and chit chat in the room. "Listen up everybody!" a man with a lit cigarette in his mouth said. "We've been given the signal to cross the border tonight at 11:00 pm. The two gentlemen next to me and I will be your guides." He avoided using the word *coyote*, but we all knew that's what he meant. Coyotes never referred to themselves as such because they had such a bad reputation.

At least four people in the group were attempting to cross the border for the second time. They had tried crossing a couple of months earlier and were chased by both the U.S. and Mexican border patrols. After getting lost in the desert for weeks, they had finally made it back to the shanty town.

The coyote reminded us to leave all our belongings behind and to remove anything that may indicate that we were not Mexican, including clothing or shoes with tags saying "Made in Peru" or El Salvador or any other country. That way, if anyone was caught, they would be released in Mexico and not deported to another country. With much sadness, I looked at the nice light blue suit that I had worn for my interview at the U.S. Embassy in Lima. I had worn it at the airport in Lima, too. Now, it was time to throw it and my backpack into the pile on the living room floor. I knew I wouldn't have money to buy clothes for a while, so I wore two pairs of pants, two t-shirts (one of which was my purple Washington, D.C. t-shirt), and a sweatshirt. I also tucked my leather shoes into the waist band of my pants.

The clock was ticking and 11:00 pm was rapidly approaching. The collective stress and anxiety in the room felt almost palpable. Most people were quiet and serious. A few had their eyes closed—most likely praying for protection—and a few others were still laying on the floor in an exhausted sleep.

I checked on Rosita and the boy; they said were ready, but the looks on their faces worried me. I was afraid one of them might have a panic attack, or that they would freeze during the crossing due to the trauma they had so recently experienced. They held each other tightly in a corner of the room. At that moment, I quietly promised myself to watch after them as if they were my siblings.

"Ready?" said the cigarette-smoking coyote, who I had silently nicknamed *Smokey*. "Everybody up! We start this journey together, and we finish together. We must stick together and help each other," he commanded. "If anyone is caught, you don't know anybody, you were crossing alone. Is that understood?"

"*Mosca* will be ahead of all of us all the time," he continued. *Mosca*, or Fly, was the young, athletic, brown-skinned coyote who would be our scout. His job was to run ahead of the group to make sure the coast was clear and to warn us if any U.S. or Mexican border control officials were up ahead. "We will walk in a line, single file, with me at the front. This *Stinky Pig*," he said, referring to the third coyote, "will be at the end of the line." *Stinky* added, "No smoking, flashlights, or lights of any kind! In the dark, a tiny light can be spotted from miles away." *Smokey* nodded in grudging agreement. It was obvious that there was a sort of power struggle going on between the two coyotes, judging by the subtle jabs flying back and forth and the way they talked to and about each other.

We left the house, walked through the last few blocks of the shanty town/settlement, and went into the darkness, both literally and figuratively. With heightened anxiety and alertness, we began making our way toward the border wall.

A mile and a half into the dark desert, still in Mexican territory, we were suddenly instructed to stop and drop to the ground. Mexican patrol trucks had been spotted driving with their lights off about 400 feet away. The shadow of the wall was visible about 600 feet ahead. We waited a few minutes until the border patrol vehicles left the area. When the signal was given, we all ran toward the 12-foot-high concrete wall.

That run was unlike any other in my life. It was charged with desperation, fear, panic, and the knowledge that there was no turning back. It was a run that only the risk-takers among the poor and marginalized have experienced, a run that is only attempted when the doors of the system have been firmly shut in one's face. It was a run from a world of despair to a world filled with hope. In that run, I felt the presence of my mom and dad, my siblings, and my grandparents, all running with me. Even as I ran, the impact of learning about Rosita's traumatic experience earlier that day was still fresh in my mind. My sense of care and compassion for Rosita, her son Pedro, and the many strangers I was with, had grown immensely that day, forever changing my life. My attitude had shifted. I was no longer just an individual chasing the American Dream. Instead, I felt like I had become a first responder/humanitarian who was working the midnight shift at the border. During the seemingly eternal 2-minute run, I saw a heavyset Salvadoran woman in her 40s drop to the ground, unable to continue. She was exhausted and breathing hard. "I can't, I can't, I can't!" she kept repeating. Two other people were trying to lift her, but her body was giving up; she had very little energy left. God knows what she had gone through on her journey from El Salvador, or what traumas she had endured during the ongoing civil war in her home country. "We can't leave you here!" I said. The three of us used our combined strength to lift her up. Two of the men pulled her by each hand, while I pushed from behind to keep the pace at a run. We were like soldiers in a battle, running to the safe zone.

Mosca had piled up some rocks in front of the wall a few minutes before to help us climb the wall. The wall still looked incredibly tall, but two men had somehow managed to climb it by the time we arrived. They sat on the edge of the wall and helped pull people up while we pushed them from below. It was a true communal effort by a group of strangers in the dark. I kept an eye on Rosita and Pedro. They seemed to be doing ok, so far. Once we crossed to the other side of the wall, the coyotes counted us. There were 33 people. "Yeah, we are all here," one of them said. We continued walking single file for about two hours through a semi-desert area, though it was hard to see it in the dark. I noticed that *Mosca* ran back from up ahead in the dark several times to give the other coyotes an update on the path ahead. We switched directions several times, following the intel that *Mosca* provided from scouting the area.

At the head of the line, *Smokey* decided to light up a cigarette. "Are you out of your mind?!" *Stinky* whispered loudly from the end of the line, confronting his partner. "I can smoke whenever and wherever I want, *hijo de la chingada*," responded *Smokey* defiantly. "Put the cigarette out right now, you hear?" *Stinky* demanded, getting into *Smokey*'s face. "I am the boss here!" "No, *I* am the boss here!"

There was no mistaking their power struggle now. Just when the fight was about to get physical, we heard the soft woosh of a helicopter. Everyone froze, and the altercation stopped almost instantly. Everyone focused intently on the wooshing sound, trying to pinpoint where it was coming from. A subtle echo in the sky confused our senses, and no one could tell for sure. *Mosca* was not around, and we were all bunched up in a treeless area. The sound from the chopper's blades suddenly increased, and we saw a spotlight beaming down from the sky along with the relentless sound—*tucu tucu tucu!* We ran to the only nearby tree that was large enough to hide under. As we rushed to the tree, the sound and spotlight were almost on top of us as the chopper circled the area. Total panic took over. We looked like rabbits, running in all directions, trying to escape the noise and swirling dust. I heard people crying, some calling out the names of relatives, as everyone ran for their lives.

Some people who had at first hidden under the tree, ran toward some bushes that were about 100 feet away. I, too, decided to run toward the bushes once I realized how obvious the tree was as a hiding spot and how vulnerable we were there. The chopper's sound was deafening, the blinding light with the swirling tornado-like dust prevented us from seeing where the chopper was or who was in it. Was it just one pilot? Or an entire swat team? I imagined the worst, sure that any second, machine guns would start shooting at us from the sky and commandos would descend to finish off anyone who had survived. I knew that dozens of people died every year crossing the Rio Grande, from exhaustion in the desert, at the hands of criminals or American militia, or in accidents. Most deaths went unreported, as the bodies were rarely found or identified. The border was a kind of "no-man's land," to say the least.

In the turbulent scenario, I managed to get a glimpse of the chopper. It was so close that strangely, the sight made me shift from flight mode to fight mode as a crazy scene from the movie, *Rambo: First Blood*, flashed in my memory. The flashback put me into *first responder mode*, and I pushed thoughts about myself aside and ran out from my hiding spot to rescue Rosita and Pedro.

I found Pedro under the tree, but his mom wasn't with him. I picked him up carried him on my shoulders as I ran toward the bushes, grabbing the hand of another older lady on my way and pulling her along, too. I went back to the tree a second time to pull more people toward the bushes because the chopper was right over the tree. By then, my only mission was to prevent a potential massacre. I rescued a few more people, returned to the bushes, and waited. The chopper circled the tree for maybe 30 seconds (which felt like hours) and then, it mysteriously took off without ever touching down or firing any bullets! I waited about five minutes after it had gone, and only then did I find Rosita, panicked, crying, and shaking in her hiding spot in the bushes.

Looking back, I wondered if the pilot had any idea of the trauma we experienced in that thunderous moment. That episode left scars in me that lasted more than two decades. Even after I was fully documented many years later, I occasionally still had nightmares, flashbacks, hyper-alertness, and mistrust of people in uniform. To this day, I wonder how Rosita, her son Pedro, and many other people dealt with the compounded traumas they experienced prior to crossing the border. How many immigrants go on living with untreated post-traumatic stress disorder (PTSD)?[4]

We walked to a safer area and rested for a few minutes. The coyotes had disappeared during the traumatic chopper incident. Their top priority was obviously to protect their own butts, not the people who had entrusted their lives to them. When they finally returned to our group, they, too, sounded scared. But at least they had finally managed to put their differences aside and work together. Following their lead, we ran, walked, and sometimes crawled for three more hours.

At around 4:30 am, we began to see specks of light on the horizon. The light came from the first homes we encountered on the American side. Just outside that first neighborhood, the coyotes divided us into groups, and we waited in the bushes for taxis to takes us to a house. Once the signal was given, seven of us ran to a taxicab that was parked in a nearby parking lot.

The taxicab had to look as if it was giving a ride to only a couple of people, so two people sat in the back seat and five of us squeezed into the trunk. We were instructed not to respond if the car stopped and someone asked something like, "Are you doing ok back there?" Luckily, nothing like that happened, and we arrived at our destination without any problems. Within a couple of hours, the entire group from the house in the shantytown the night before was reunited

---

[4] Post-traumatic stress disorder (PTSD) is a mental health condition triggered by experiencing or witnessing a traumatic event. It involves symptoms like flashbacks, nightmares, severe anxiety, and uncontrollable thoughts about the event. PTSD can significantly impact daily life and relationships.

in the garage of an American townhouse. Except we were no longer the same people we had been just 12 hours earlier. Every single person looked exhausted and at least 10 years older. Everyone was covered in mud and dust, and some had bruises, scratches, and ripped clothing from the barbed wire we had encountered while traversing a few ranches in the dark along the way. The smell of sweat and feet was nothing compared to the sense of relief we all felt at being safe and alive.

At around noon, one of the owners of the townhouse introduced himself to the group and brought three buckets filled with fried chicken. I recognized the brand—Kentucky Fried Chicken. It was the same logo I had seen plastered over buckets in the movies. Every piece of chicken in the buckets disappeared in no time, and I made sure that Rosita and Pedro both had enough.

A couple of hours later, several large all-American Lincoln and Ford taxicabs arrived at the townhouse, one by one, to avoid raising suspicions. They came to transport the merchandize (i.e., us!) to a motel close to downtown Los Angeles. I was luckier this time because they told me to ride in the back seat, so I didn't have to squeeze into yet another trunk. As I got into the Lincoln, I had a flashback to one of the great Western movies. The driver looked just like Clint Eastwood! He had the same height, body type, skin tone, and haircut, and he wore the trademark cowboy hat, vest, and pointy boots. Even his personality screamed "cowboy!" and to me, it was him. I would have sworn it!

With a cigar clamped between his lips, *Clint* remained silent throughout the entire journey, his expression stoic. Yet, with him behind the wheel, the ride to the next budget motel took on an unexpected air of excitement, adding a touch of intrigue to our adventure. *Clint* drove as I imagined a real, cool, modern American Cowboy would drive—fast but calm—along the immense Los Angeles highways. He drove with supreme confidence, orchestrating every lane change with the ease that comes from experience. It was a real treat to get to observe him in his element. Much as I admired *Clint's* calm demeanor, it shocked me a little to see a white guy doing such a risky job and living like I imagined a modern Western Cowboy would live—an outlaw doing business with his frenemies, the Mexican *bandidos* (bandits).

We reached our destination, and *Clint* had still not spoken a single word. I felt like I was simultaneously watching and starring in a Western movie. *Clint* gracefully maneuvered the Lincoln into its designated spot, then alighted from the vehicle with an aura of composed assurance. With a subtle yet commanding gesture, he beckoned to us to disembark and proceed toward the awaiting motel. Part of me wanted to ask for an autograph, but instead, I turned around and watched as the Mexican *bandido* came out from the motel and shook his hand. *Clint* pocketed the wad of cash he had received with the handshake, got back into his Lincoln, and rode off into the sunset.

Later that night, people were dispatched to buses or planes, one by one, on route to their final destinations. There was no time for proper goodbyes. Everyone simply disappeared to their own destiny. When it was my turn, one of the guides gave me a ride to the airport. He instructed me on how to check in and board the plane, and then left me at the airport entrance. I never saw Rosita or Pedro again, but I think about them often, even today, when I work with clients

who have experienced sexual traumas or who have been mistreated.

Photo 2. My older brother and I playing cowboys in our backyard. Hollywood's Western movies inspired children's games since the 1950s.

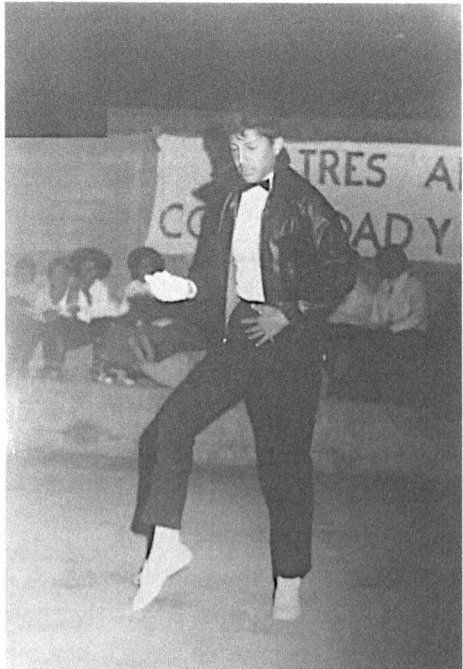

Photo 3. A Michael Jackson look-a-like performing *Billie Jean* at a community event. Peru, 1984. *Photo courtesy of Raul Thomas Pinto.*

CHAPTER 3

The Immigrant Without

"The Eagle from the North welcomes the Condor from the South"

~ Chief Joseph Raincrow Neale

I arrived in Washington, D.C. a couple of days after a big snowstorm in 1987, and I wasn't prepared for winter at all—I didn't even have proper clothes, just what I was wearing when I had crossed the border. I also didn't have any money to buy things, not even food. At first, I relied on spare change from my roommates to get by. The day after moving into my aunt's apartment, I sat in the empty room feeling lost and alone. I thought about my family and all the things I'd lost. I felt like an alien in this place where almost nobody knew or cared about me. That morning, my roommate had forgotten his Walkman on the bed when he left for work. Curious, I put on the head set and pressed the play button, and I'll never forget the song that came out on. It was like it was written just for me:

He's a real nowhere man
Sitting in his nowhere land

Making all his nowhere plans for nobody

Doesn't have a point of view
Knows not where he's going to
Isn't he a bit like you and me?

Nowhere man, please listen
You don't know what you're missing
Nowhere man, the world is at your command

He's as blind as he can be
Just sees what he wants to see
Nowhere man, can you see me at all

Nowhere man, don't worry
Take your time, don't hurry
Leave it all 'til somebody else
Lends you a hand... Ah, la, la, la, la...

He's a real nowhere man
Sitting in his nowhere land
Making all his nowhere plans for nobody
Making all his nowhere plans for nobody
Making all his nowhere plans for nobody
Making all his nowhere plans for nobody[1]

~ John Lennon and Paul McCartney

Even though I didn't understand all the lyrics of that Beatles'
hit song, something about the music hit me hard, and I listened to it over and over as I cried, feeling a deep hole in my
soul. The song became impregnated into my being, and to
this day, it transports me back to those early days in 1987.

---

[1] Lyrics of the song, *Nowhere Man* by the Beatles (1965). On *Rubber Soul* [Album]. Parlophone.

As days passed, I became increasingly concerned about my lack of income. I asked my roommate and aunt to reach out to their networks and offered to take any job that paid minimum wage or even less. Aunt Juana, who now worked as a banquet server in downtown Washington, D.C., pledged to help. She knew that my undocumented status wasn't helping my job hunt. One day, she took me to a temporary agency[2] in downtown D.C. that was known for placing workers in low-skilled jobs.

I had never heard of temp agencies, and I was nervous about using them to find a job. Aunt Juana stayed in the waiting room while I went inside for a short screening interview and paperwork. I was both surprised and relieved to discover that the secretary spoke some Spanish. She explained they were primarily hiring dishwashers, and I eagerly expressed my interest in that job. I asked to be considered for other tasks, too, like cleaning or mopping the floors. Both jobs were in high demand, since most Americans weren't interested in that kind of work. Because I was desperate for a job, I avoided mentioning my documentation status. But the secretary had probably guessed the situation from my demeanor and eagerness to take on pretty much any work. As if reading my mind, she asked for my social security card. I froze and my mind went blank for a couple

---

[2] A temporary agency in the kitchen or hotel cleaning industry is a company that provides businesses with temporary or short-term cleaning staff. These agencies specialize in recruiting and managing workers who are available to fill in for permanent staff, handle peak periods, or cover for absences. They handle the hiring, training, and payroll for these workers, allowing hotels and kitchens to maintain cleanliness and operations without the long-term commitment of hiring permanent employees.

of seconds, but I quickly gathered my thoughts and told her that I didn't have the card with me right then, but I could write down the number. Thankfully, she said, "Okay. Write down the number, and when you have a chance, bring me the card so I can make a copy of it." I said I would. *Uff, that was close!* Walking in and out of the shadows to survive often requires immigrants to compromise their morals, and I was no exception. Making up a social security number felt wrong, of course, but not doing it meant starvation, homelessness, or worse. Taking this step increased the fear and shame that had become my constant companions on this journey.

A few minutes after handing in my application, the secretary at the temp agency hired me on the spot. She instructed me to report to a hotel in three hours for my first job as a dishwasher at a large dinner-dance event in downtown D.C. I was so thrilled that you'd have thought I'd landed a position as CEO of a major corporation! After the weeks-long search, finally getting a job, even a temporary one, really lifted my spirits. I felt an unfamiliar surge of excitement and optimism.

The temporary agency was known for helping recent immigrants, and the fact that many of us were undocumented was never spoken aloud. This help came with a price, however, which was that we had to follow an unwritten rule: Accept everything without complaint or risk being reported to the immigration authorities (U.S. Immigration and Naturalization Service, or INS),[3] not so affectionately known as "La

---

[3] The U.S. Immigration and Naturalization Service (INS) was an agency of the U.S. Department of Justice, it ceased to exist under that name on March 1, 2003. Most of its functions were transferred to the U.S. Immigration and Customs Enforcement (ICE) within the newly

Migra".[4] Because we immigrants truly depended on these temporary jobs for survival, the agency held monopoly-like power in D.C.'s hospitality industry, and they used it to their advantage. They had the reputation of hiring young people and expecting them to work hard for long hours, including on holidays, often with little or no prior notice before starting jobs. The agency also extracted taxes from our paychecks just like any other employer (yes, you read that right—many undocumented immigrants actually pay taxes); but they also took full advantage of our lack of legal status by subtracting fees for benefits we could never use for fear of getting caught.

The harder you worked, the more they liked you, and if they didn't like you, you were "expendable." Soon after starting, I realized I needed to find a way to become part of their group of favorite workers, which I secretly thought of as the "VIP dishwashers club." That meant showing them that I had to be ready to work—and work hard—whenever they called, even if it was at the last minute. Often, I had to show up to work very early or return home after the city buses had stopped running, so long walks along the dark streets of Washington, D.C. became my new norm. I certainly hadn't expected to work so hard for so little pay in America, but

---

created Department of Homeland Security (DHS), as part of a major government reorganization following the September 11 attacks of 2001.

[4] La "Migra" is a colloquial term used by some Latinx communities to refer to U.S. immigration enforcement agencies, such as Immigration and Customs Enforcement (ICE) or Customs and Border Protection (CBP). The term has historical roots and is often used in informal contexts to discuss immigration authorities and their activities. It can carry a range of connotations, from neutral to negative, depending on the context in which it is used.

with so many debts to pay in Peru, there was no choice. My family was counting on me.

Me No Habla English

By the time I arrived in D.C., I had forgotten most of the rudimentary English that I'd learned in high school. Carrying on even a basic conversation was next to impossible, but I used my admiration for the Beatles to at least try to understand the lyrics of their hit songs. Unfortunately, the Beatles didn't write lyrics about how to do a job search; that would have been helpful! Despite my "disability," I found myself walking down Wisconsin Avenue toward Georgetown on a chilly morning, looking for "Help Wanted" signs. Seeing such a sign in the window at a small "mom and pop" grocery store, I stopped and hesitated, realizing that I didn't know what to say. I knew the verb "work" in English, and that was about it. But then I thought, *maybe they just need someone to work in the back who doesn't need to speak English, and maybe they need help so badly that they won't even ask for documents.*

I took a deep breath, screwed up my courage, and went inside the store. The person behind the counter looked to be the manager, so I said, "Good morning." "I" [pointing at my chest] "work," I continued haltingly, nodding and pointing at the floor, gesturing, "here?" The manager said something, but what? My mind did its best to decode what she said, but I'd maxed out my English vocabulary. It was as if the manager had just talked to me in some alien language. (Ironic that to me, she seemed like the alien!) I didn't want to look confused, so I smiled and repeated "I work" a couple of times. Finally, I heard the manager say, "Sorry." And she looked sorry, too, so I figured I didn't get the job. I thanked her and left the grocery store, feeling like a complete mute and looking for a bush to hide under. Later that day, I bought a dictionary and decided to learn English, one word at a time.

As a sociable teenager, I had excelled at making positive first impressions when speaking my native language—an invaluable skill during my days as a street vendor in Peru. However, my outgoing nature clashed with my struggle to adapt socially, particularly with English speakers. I wanted to have meaningful conversations, but my language barrier posed a significant challenge. Occasionally, I found myself attracted to the girls I met in different places, but my inability to communicate effectively left me feeling frustrated and unable to express myself. That frustration pushed me relentlessly to learn English. I spent all my spare time memorizing phrases, practicing my accent, or watching English-language news or movies, even if I didn't understand everything. Overcoming the language barrier became my next border to cross, and I was determined to cross it. It wasn't easy, though, and I had to be super disciplined. Not only because everyone in the apartment spoke Spanish, but also because I had so little spare time.

For weeks, I took all the worst dishwashing shifts and worked until utter exhaustion in order to earn a pass into the "VIP dishwashers club." In addition to dishwashing, which became my "secure" full-time job, I took on occasional part-time jobs like painting or doing yard work. I worked in all sorts of places—some greasy, dark, or steamy, and others chaotic—often at hotels or restaurants. Some of my bosses were nice and others weren't, but I generally said "yes" to every job, big or small. In part, because I needed the money, but also because saying "no" would require me to provide an explanation, which I couldn't really do with such basic English skills.

My roommate, Franco, who had arrived in Washington, D.C. 10 months before me, encouraged me to take English classes at the Georgetown High School program for adult immigrants. It didn't take much convincing. As soon as I had a relatively stable schedule, I registered for the classes. At the school, I met immigrants from all over the world. At first, I couldn't communicate much with anyone, but at least it was nice to see so many other people who were also new to the American experience. With the addition of English class, my daily routine during those first few months was: work all night starting at 6 pm, walk back home at dawn, sleep until 2 pm, eat a quick breakfast, attend English class from 3-5 pm, and catch the bus to start work all over again at 6 pm. On the days when we didn't have class, I worked as a janitor at a private school. On Saturdays, I worked at odd jobs, mostly as a helper.

Holy Sundays

Sundays were my only days off, and I reserved them for the Lord. A few weeks after my arrival in Washington, D.C., I joined *Nuestra Señora de las Americas* (Our Lady of the Americas) Catholic Church, located a few blocks from the Washington Hilton Hotel, where I often worked. As I became involved with the church, I got to know Brother Jaime, the charismatic Peruvian seminarian who directed the choir. He had a 12-string acoustic guitar, and he knew how to play it.

His energy made singing in the choir exciting, and the entire congregation responded enthusiastically to his musical direction.

One chilly Sunday, Brother Jaime noticed that while everyone else in the choir had heavy jackets, scarves, and mittens, I only had a thin sweater. He said, "You must be freezing, Ricardo, where is your coat?" "I don't have winter clothing or a coat," I said, "I am new to this country." He pulled me aside and walked me across the hallway to another room in the building. He opened the door and said, "Take what you need." The room was filled with a huge pile of donated winter clothes that were going to be distributed to low-income families in Washington, D.C. Grateful, I took a few warm clothes, mittens, and a blanket, which I used for several years.

I found a sense of belonging at church and formed friendships that made the choir feel like home. The Central American, South American, and Mexican choir members shared backgrounds like mine. Nearly everyone was a recent immigrant, and some were undocumented, like me. Most worked at low-wage jobs in restaurants or construction, and some had cleaning jobs. Others, often mothers who'd been forced to leave their own children with relatives in their home countries, worked as nannies, taking care of American children. Our Sunday gatherings weren't just about singing for church services; they were opportunities for us to connect with each other and build friendships. After Sunday services finished, our time together didn't end. We often lingered until 10:00 pm or even later, cherishing the chance to chat, sing, swap stories, laugh, and sometimes, shed tears. We celebrated each other's birthdays, and we gathered in the church basement or someone's apartment to watch movies. Our weekdays were hectic, filled with work pressures, the strain of adapting to a new culture, and for some, the challenge of parenting from afar. But Sundays? Sundays were our sanctuary, our slice of heaven on Earth. They were the only day of the week when we could truly be ourselves, accepted and cared for by our tight-knit choir family.

Having learned how to play the guitar in Peru, one day, I showed up at church with a new guitar that I had bought at a yard sale. I joined Brother Jaime and two other guitarists, adding string melodies to our songs while the singers experimented with vocal harmonies. Shortly thereafter, another guitarist and a charangoist (a charango is an Andean banjo-like instrument with double the number of strings) emerged from the group. I often played my Peruvian flute, called a *quena*, too, switching from one instrument to the other. Since I didn't have a guitar case, I walked through the hallways with my guitar strapped to my back. That earned me the nickname, "Ritchie Valens," when the movie *La Bamba* was released later that year. My friends told me I was Ritchie's look-a-like. Being called "Ritchie" made me feel important and appreciated, as if I had fans. It boosted my confidence, which was nice after feeling like an exploited, unappreciated, "no-where man" dishwasher the rest of the week.

On one of those wonderful Sundays, a beautiful lady in the choir confessed that she had a crush on me. Her name was Maria, and she was a 23-year-old single mother who had migrated from Chile two years before me. I was so young and naïve that I didn't know what to do. I had been so focused on helping my family make ends meet that I had had little time for boyfriend/girlfriend stuff in Peru. Plus, I had attended an all-boys school in Peru, so I had little experience dealing with girls. Luckily, Maria understood my confusion and did not make fun of me. We agreed to take it slow, and I was glad we did, because it turned out to be just a mild attraction that later developed into a great friendship, nothing else.

Maria had made the tough decision to leave her impoverished community to secure a better future for her 3-year-old daughter. Because she overstayed her visa in the U.S. due to economic struggles, she was unable to return to Chile to visit her daughter or her family. She worked as a nanny for a white middle-class family, and they adored her because she did everything for them. She cleaned the house, did the cooking, and took care of the children, walking them to and from school and teaching them Spanish. The children had even begun to call her "mom," but the loved she received from her American 'family' compounded the pain she felt for having left her own daughter. Her American family filed a petition for a work visa for Maria, but it had been waitlisted for over five years. Most of Maria's salary went to her parents in Chile to pay for food and schooling for her daughter and her family. Not surprisingly, Maria suffered from depression and cried herself to sleep every night. Often, she came to church with her eyes reddened from crying. Sometimes when she didn't come to church, we went to the home where she worked to cheer her up.

As heart wrenching as Maria's story was, it was sadly run-of-the-mill from my perspective as an immigrant. Most people can't imagine voluntarily abandoning their children, but immigrants (i.e., illegal aliens, as some people say) often have no choice. Either we leave our children to get work and earn money, or all of us would starve or become victims of gangs, criminals, or even the military or police. Unfortunately, we're vulnerable no matter where we go, including the U.S.

Aliens Can See... But Not Report

Individuals who report crimes or domestic violence are typically required to provide their names and other personal information, and their phone numbers and locations may also be traceable. But as any immigrant knows, that information can be used against you. Employers know this, too, of course, and some of them use this knowledge to exploit undocumented workers by paying less than minimum wage, demanding long hours, disallowing overtime pay, and sometimes, not paying at all. Most get away with this because undocumented people basically have no rights. According to the Economic Policy institute, between 2017-2020 low-wage workers, many of whom are immigrants, lose up to 15% of their annual earnings due to wage theft. But these figures represent only a fraction of the actual wage theft occurring across the country.

The abuses that immigrants endure aren't just financial, and they don't only affect the undocumented. Once, I witnessed police brutality at around 4 am, when my roommate and I were walking home from work. Two police officers were beating a black man who was handcuffed against a police car. It was the first time I had witnessed such a disturbing scene in the U.S., and I wanted to say something to stop the beating. Fear of repercussions kept me from intervening or saying anything to stop the violence. Instead, I crossed to the other side of the street and continued walking, feeling both scared and impotent.

Another time, I witnessed domestic violence in a home where I had been renting a room with a couch that had served as my bed. The person who became violent was a legal resident, while his partner was undocumented. The first time they fought, I pretended to be asleep and didn't get involved. The couple screamed at each other in their bedroom, and I heard sounds as if someone was being thrown against the wall and the door. I wanted to call the police, but again, I couldn't do anything. Fortunately, the fight ended when the husband slammed the door, left the apartment, and went to his car. The next day, I saw big bruises on the wife's face, neck, and arms. I asked why she didn't call the police, but she said she was afraid they would find out she was undocumented, and she didn't want anybody to be arrested. Plus, she believed that if she called the police, they would only listen to her partner because he spoke English, and she did not.

A few weeks later, when everyone was asleep, the husband came home drunk. Another fight broke out and this time, the physical abuse did not stop. I wanted to scare him, so I knocked on the door and, with some apprehension, said, "Hey! Stop the fight now, or I will call the police!" The husband was furious when he came out of the room to confront me. He threatened to call "La Migra" if I called the police. I was terrified, so I quickly shut my mouth. But at least my disruption made him stop beating his wife. After yelling at me a little more, he walked out of the house and went to his car. I was scared that he might do something to get back at me, though, so the next morning, I moved out.

A couple of years later, I found out that the wife eventually left the abusive relationship. But by then, she had a one-year-old baby girl who probably had to grow up without a father. How different would her life have been if she had been able to report the domestic abuse earlier, without fear of being deported?[5] These are just a few examples that I've seen personally; it's impossible to say how many similar stories have played out where people had to stay quiet.[6]

Where Are You, Mama?

Like most kids, when I was little, I took for granted that my parents would come to my rescue when I was sick or needed comforting. But during my first year in America, I felt a profound hole in my chest when I was in physical or emotional pain because my mother's caring support was missing. It was like a child's pain. I missed the cold wet cloths that my mom would put on my forehead to ease a high fever, the herbs that she would steep in hot water to heal my stomach or throat pain, and most of all, her healing presence by my bedside. *I left home too early*, I thought, *I need you, mama, but you are not here.* Instead, I often turned to my mother's herbal teas and home remedies to stay healthy. As

---

[5] U.S. law provides several protections for legal and undocumented immigrants who have been victims of a crime. There are specific protections for victims of domestic violence, victims of certain crimes, and victims of human trafficking. More information: https://www.dhs.gov/immigration-options-victims-crime

[6] If you or someone is a victim of domestic violence, help is available. Speak with someone today by calling the National Domestic Violence Hotline 800-799-7233. The service is available 24/7 in English, Spanish and 200+ languages through interpretation service.

an undocumented worker, I had no access to medical insurance. I agreed with all the other recent immigrants, who often said, "we're not allowed to get sick."

Often, my knees would ache from standing for hours and my wrists, hands, and feet would swell from being in hot, steamy spaces for 14 to 18 hours per day, washing dishes and scrubbing pans. One day, when my knees were killing me, I "sacrificed" my Washington, D.C. t-shirt to make "bandages" for my knees and wrists. The letters and image of Capitol Hill were almost gone anyway, and the purple color had faded to a sweat-stained yellowish gray. The bandages from the shirt and some generic muscle rub temporarily took care of my joint pain.

Sometimes, the pain was sharper and not so easy to alleviate. One day when I was walking to work, I suddenly felt a sharp pain in my pelvic area. The pain was so unbearable that I could not walk. I fell to my knees, beyond scared. *Would I pass out and die on the street?* I thought as I started to panic. Somehow, I managed to stand up and walk to the nearest alley to check the afflicted area. I was bleeding through the urethral opening. The pain was excruciating, so intense that I wanted to scream. *Mom, I need help!!!* Bent almost in half from pain, I limped back to the sidewalk and took a taxi back home. The next two days I spent in bed, trying to resist the pain and praying it would go away. My mind conjured up the worst possible scenarios. I thought I had cancer or some other incurable disease. Or maybe I had contracted AIDS,[7] the incurable disease that everyone was

---

[7] AIDS (Acquired Immunodeficiency Syndrome) is the advanced stage of HIV infection, where the immune system is severely weakened. AIDS was first identified in the early 1980s, primarily affecting gay men

talking about in the 1980s. I was scared to death that I was going to die, so I kept telling myself, *don't die now! I can't die alone, away from home.* I was truly in a panic. *I haven't paid my debts! My family would be thrown into the streets of Peru!*

Finally, I called a Peruvian man who spoke English to ask for help. I had just met him a few weeks ago. He helped me find a bilingual internal medicine physician and he took me to the doctor's office. The doctor who saw me happened to be a Latino from Colombia. He said that I had a urinary tract infection, and it was curable. All the stuff I'd created in my mind about cancer and AIDS disappeared, and I was flooded with relief. "What type of work do you do, Ricardo?" he asked. I said I was a dishwasher, and I worked long hours. "How often do you go to the bathroom?" he continued. "Only on my break," I replied, "it's the only time I am allowed to leave my spot by the industrial dishwashing machine." He prescribed antibiotics and recommended that I listen to my body. "You can't hold urine in your bladder for too long if you want to prevent future infections," he said. "If you have to pee, you have to pee! A good boss will understand." I explained my legal and economic situation to the doctor, and compassionately, he agreed to treat me at no cost. Within a couple of days, I was back on my feet.

Of course, I never breathed a word about any of these experiences to my family. Phone calls were super expensive, so I stayed connected with my family, especially my mother, via written correspondence. In my letters, I told her how beautiful life was in America, and I wrote about my good experiences while hiding the painful ones. The last thing I

---

and IV drug users. It led to a global epidemic, prompting widespread public health efforts and medical advancements in treatment.

wanted was to make my mother worry, so I never wrote about things like police brutality, domestic violence, or medical emergencies. I also didn't tell her about my first Mother's Day without her.

Mothers' Day of 1987 was one of the most difficult days I experienced in America. I went to the Spanish-speaking service at Saint Anthony's Catholic church in Arlington. The mid-size church was packed with Central American families, including many well-dressed mothers and grandmothers. Some were holding flowers that their family members had given them. I was very sad because my mother and family were not next to me. During communion, all the mothers in the room started to line up to receive communion. The line was about 50 feet away, and when I looked at it, I suddenly saw Mama Betty—I swear it was her—making her way up the line! I couldn't believe it! I quickly stood up, wanting to call out her name from across the aisle… *"Mama Betty!!!"* Instead, I softly said, "*disculpe*" (excuse me) to excuse myself as I urgently made my way toward her, pushing past the people who were seated in my pew. She had the same hairstyle, skin tone, height, and weight as she had when I'd left home. I was about 10 feet away when she finally turned around. My entire being wanted nothing more than to see Mama Betty, but the lady I saw was not my mother. My hopes were dashed; I felt a stab in my heart. The disappointment was too great to hold. I couldn't bring myself to go back to my seat. Instead, I walked to the parking lot and cried until there were no tears left. "*Where are you, mamita?*" I said over and over again. Although I was 18 and felt ready to be out in the world as a grown man, I didn't realize how emotionally attached I was to my mom. I missed her terribly, but I couldn't be with her.

The first six months in America were the most difficult. The hardest part wasn't physical or mental, it was emotional. I worried constantly about my siblings and my parents. Not knowing when I would see them again was beyond painful, and I spent many nights crying silently. Every airplane I saw flying overhead made me sad. Airplanes were constant reminders of the distance between myself and everything and everyone I had left behind. On occasional days off, I purposely rode on the Metrorail from one end of the city to the other for hours, just daydreaming about being with my siblings and friends. I longed for the good old days in Peru, and I thought about life's cruel ironies, remembering how desperately I had wanted to emigrate to America while I was growing up in Peru. Of course, the America I had wanted to migrate to was the Hollywood version. Now, I saw that the American Dream that had been exported to Peru and elsewhere was a lie. After risking my life to come to this land, I realized that I was not welcome here. I felt cheated, unloved, and vulnerable in the country of my dreams.

For a while, I turned to drinking to numb the pain of these feelings. After work, I drank in the park with other immigrants. Most of the time, our conversations started pleasantly enough, with comradery and jokes. But before long, we often ended up crying as we shared our sorrows and pain. Occasionally, I just drank and cried alone in my room, listening to sad romantic ballads and reminiscing about my past in Peru. Paradoxically, my thoughts about the "good old days in Peru" included many American influences, from pop music to films watched in Peruvian movie theaters, childhood games of cowboys and indians, breakdancing, and countless other American-influenced activities.

One day, one of my friends was caught by the police drinking while walking home from "our" park. After a few days, we found out that he had been detained and deported. I was sad that he had been deported. He was a good man, and I knew about his struggles, his history of family abuse, and his burning desire to help his younger siblings. The incident was a wake-up call for me. Despite my depression, I stopped drinking in public places. Drinking was not going to help me or my family, I realized. Plus, I couldn't stop thinking, *if something happens to me, who will help my family?*

Angels and Nature Spirits to the Rescue

Have you ever seen an angel? I believe angels show up in life unexpectedly when you need them, maybe as spirits, people, animals, or events. Sometimes, they come to impart indelible life lessons, and they can show up anywhere, even at work.

One day, I noticed a cute Salvadorian girl named Yolanda who also worked as a dishwasher. She looked to be my age. After seeing her a few times in the cafeteria, I got up the courage to ask if I could join her at the table. Yolanda agreed and we chatted over our lunch break. After several of these encounters, our attraction to each other grew until one day after work, we kissed passionately outside the hotel where we both worked. I asked Yolanda if I could visit her at her place the following day, and she agreed. She said, "Be there at 4 pm. Not before or after, ok?" I enthusiastically promised to be on time. I went home dreaming about holding her in my arms, watching sunsets together, and starting our life together in this new country.

I arrived at Yolanda's apartment about 20 minutes after 4 pm. We kissed hello at the door, and I went inside. "You are late," she said. "Yes, I'm sorry, I missed my bus and had to wait for the next one, but here I am, and these flowers are for you," I responded, handing her the carnations I had purchased from an immigrant street seller. She was babysitting a cute infant, who was sitting in a highchair. "What a cute baby, Yolanda, are his parents at work?" I asked. She paused for a second. In the silence, I asked, "How often do you babysit?" Finally, she admitted, "It's my baby," watching closely for my reaction. Naïvely, I assumed that she was a single mom, which increased my appreciation for her even more. Then, I noticed that she was edgy and looked distracted, even anxious. She went to check the window as the loud sound of a Metro bus engine signaled its departure from the bus stop across the street. She ran back to the living room, and said, in a voice tinged with panic, "My husband is home! My husband is home! Hide! Go!" At first, I thought she was kidding. But then, I looked out the window and saw a guy crossing the street, walking toward the building where we were. "Shit, where do I go, what should I do!?!" In my panic, I ran around the apartment like a chicken without a head, looking for a place to hide. *The closet? No, too obvious! Under the bed? No, you could see under it from the door! The window? Nooo!* Quickly, I grabbed my backpack and rushed out of the apartment just in time.

As I walked down the hallway, pretending to be calm as my heart raced at full speed, I passed the guy who was walking toward the apartment I had just left. I looked at him and kept walking as naturally as possible. I didn't dare wait for the elevator. Instead, I took the stairs and left the building as fast as I could. Needless to say, I was terrified. In the short time I'd been in the U.S., I had heard many stories about Salvadoran *macheteros* (butchers), who were known to take justice into their own hands, hunting people down and leaving them to bleed to death. The civil war in El Salvador had been going on for ten years, and the stories of brutal encounters with *macheteros* were haunting. During the war, peasants and farmers used machetes as their main weapon to defend themselves from guerrillas or the Salvadoran army. I had also heard that the *'machetero within'* would come out when a Salvadoran found out that his woman was cheating on him, even in Washington, D.C.

I learned two very important life lessons that day. One, make sure the woman you're courting isn't married or in a relationship before you start courting her! And two, I can get out of a life-threatening situation pretty darn quickly when I have to, which could come in handy in the event of an immigration raid or another emergency. I was disappointed that I'd wasted money on an expensive bouquet of flowers. But maybe it was a small price to pay for the lessons that I think my angel was trying to convey: Stay alert, don't just follow hormonal impulses, scan the environment, and look for exit routes in case of emergency.

Can Gringos Be Angels?

Late one afternoon, after a long day's work at a downtown hotel, I was seated at a bus stop, waiting for the bus and gazing at the sunset when suddenly, a tennis ball rolled by my feet. I picked it up, turned it around, and realized that a middle-age white man was waving at me from a tennis court, signaling to toss the ball back to him. There was a wire fence between us, and I didn't want to throw the ball because if it hit the fence, I would have to run to get it again. Instead, I walked toward him. We met halfway, and I handed the ball to him. He received the ball graciously and said, "thank you," quickly followed by, "Que patria por tu?" (Where are you from?) in his best Spanglish. I reciprocated his friendly greeting, using my best basic English, "bery good, bery good, and you, mister?" As we struggled to put together a conversation with our limited English/Spanish vocabularies, I heard the roaring engine of my bus leaving the bus stop without me. Part of me wanted to run after the bus, but that would have been impolite. Plus, he was one of the first *real* Americans who seemed like he wanted to be my friend. Realizing that I would have to wait 40 more minutes, I accepted his invitation to play tennis until the next bus arrived. "My name is John," he said. "Like John Travolta?" I asked. "Yes," he responded. "Me no play tennis before, mister," I said. "No problema, amigo, I teach you the basico." He showed me how to hold and swing the tennis racket, and we played for a few minutes until the next bus came.

We ran into each other a few more times after that at the same bus stop. Initially, I wasn't sure if I should hang out with him. I was skeptical of everyone—especially white American men. *What if this guy is an undercover immigration officer or an FBI agent?* I thought. *Or what if he was a psycho, trying to rob me?* With the traumas from my journey still fresh, my distrust refused to leave me alone. I had developed a law enforcement phobia and tried to keep my distance from anyone who might be an undercover agent. But John seemed too humble and friendly to be an agent. Over time, my loneliness won out over my fear, and I began to warm to John's persistent friendliness. Despite our cultural and linguistic differences and bumpy communication, our friendship began to unfold, and with it, my preconceptions about gringos began to change. We began playing tennis together and afterward, we began to hang out and chat in Spanglish.

John's journey was filled with family betrayals, greed, and disappointments, and maybe that's why he was able to empathize with my life as an immigrant. He was born into a prominent business family of English descent in the Boston area. The problems within his immediate family and among the members of his extended family were endless. They were ruthless in taking legal action against each other, which ultimately destroyed his once-happy, prosperous family. As a result, his family disintegrated when he was young. The breakup of his family affected him profoundly, skewing his views around the meaning of family, romantic relationships, and business partnerships. Tired of being involved in family dramas, he completely detached from them. He wanted nothing to do with them or their money; instead, he started a new life of his own. He moved to Washington, D.C. and worked as an independent consultant. He was self-sufficient, but he had only a handful of people he could call friends.

John clearly had his share of childhood traumas and fears. I got the feeling that once, he had had it all. But today, he wanted to live like one of us "wetbacks." Perhaps he identified with the struggles of undocumented immigrants because they reminded him of the natural, unsophisticated, humble, and honest part of himself. Like us, John lived in two worlds. During the day, he existed in the competitive, business "rat race" world, as he used to call it; and in the evenings and on weekends, he retreated to a more natural, peaceful world with his friends, most of whom were Latino immigrants.

As our friendship developed, John began to take an interest in my health and education. One day, John asked me, in his best Spanglish, "Que dreams por tu in America?" (What are your dreams, now that you are in America?) Using my own Spanglish, I told him that I was here to work, to help my family, and to find my American Dream. I wanted to get a green card, go to college, become a professional, help people, have my own house, and later, have a family of my own, I continued. Then I asked, "What is your American Dream, John?" He paused for a moment as if the question was somewhat foreign to him, "My American Dream... hum... Well, I don't know what to say. I thought I lived the American Dream... but... it is getting late Ricardo, you need to get home soon," he said, changing the subject, perhaps, to avoid revisiting painful memories.

That conversation seemed to plant a seed in John's head, and from then on, he made it a goal to help me get into college. For months, he tried to get different colleges in the area to allow me to register to take at least one class, only to be rejected because of my legal status. It seemed that all college doors were closed to undocumented students. Although some American colleges valued diversity and tried to create inclusive environments, that vision usually didn't include the growing undocumented population. But John was nothing if not persistent, and he insisted that I write monthly essays summarizing the lessons I had learned from English class, work, and my interactions with people so I would be prepared for the rigors of academia. Each month, he read my essays, corrected my grammar, and wrote comments as if he were my college professor.

I don't think John was aware of the huge impact he was having on me, and I'm not just talking about my education. By observing him patiently explain the admissions process, set up appointments, and advocate for me, he was unknowingly challenging the negative stereotypes I had of whites. He was genuinely doing his best to help me get an education, and I knew that he had done the same for other undocumented immigrants. He respectfully persuaded jaded receptionists to make appointments, and he often succeeded in getting us in the door. Once we set foot in the decision maker's office, he was a master at persuasion and negotiation. During these conversations, the admissions directors were generally steadfast in their commitment to follow formal university protocols. John, on the other hand, brought forward humanistic arguments, emphasizing the true purpose of higher education, the long-term benefits for society, and the real meaning of life success. It was a treat to watch John in action. He respectfully challenged objections using the right language, gestures, and willingness to compromise while keeping an eye on the prize.

One day, a frustrated John said, "Ricardo, there must be a college that will accept you even with your current legal status," after trying in vain to help me register for a class at three different colleges. While I agreed with him, I didn't know where else to look. I had no idea how to navigate the higher education system in the United States. "There is one more school we need to check," John said. "It's a private university. Our chances are very slim, and even if they allow you to take a class, it will be very expensive," he warned.

The school he was referring to was American University (AU). After several failed attempts to make an appointment to meet with the head of the registrar's office, John and I decided to just show up with my forms and transcripts in hand. He had done this a few times before, and John knew some secrets of highly persuasive businesspeople that he put to good use. He paid attention to details such as personal attire, gestures, good grooming, and being on time and organized. He taught me the importance of making a good first impression. Initially, I thought all his strategies and preparation were a bunch of bullshit, but he told me that some people judge others, especially immigrants, by their appearance, and that made sense.

At AU, the admissions director diplomatically praised me, saying, "He sounds like a great person with novel dreams." But then, like all the others, he explained that I couldn't study there because I didn't meet the admissions requirements. John's reply was something like, "Think of your own child if he received the same response while eagerly pursuing his dream, after all the other doors had been shut in his face. What would you do?" In the end, John and the admissions officer reached a stalemate. The officer did not deny or accept my application. Instead, he said, "Since Ricardo is a recent immigrant, he could apply as an international student," strategically directing us to the International Student Services (ISS) office. "It is up to them," he said, though it was obvious by then that the officer was exasperated by John's persistence. He knew perfectly well that ISS required students to have student visas, and that I wouldn't have a chance. He just wanted us out of his office.

The Eagle Meets the Condor

We hadn't come this far to just give up. John arranged an appointment with ISS, and a couple of days later, we returned to AU. In the hallway, before our meeting, we looked at each other and agreed to accept the decision, no matter what happened. "Let's just remember that we've done our best," John said. I agreed. He straightened my tie, and we walked toward the ISS office. The name plate on the door to the office read, "Director of International Student Services – Dr. Joseph R. Neale."

"Good afternoon, Dr. Neale," I said, as we entered the office. "You must be Ricardo, how are you?" he asked. I politely replied in my best heavily accented English, "bery good, dóctor, bery good. And you?" John greeted Dr. Neale, as well. I looked around and quickly noticed it was an atypical American academic office. The wooden desk, IBM®[8] computer, and diplomas hanging on the wall were the only items that indicated it was the ISS office. The rest of the office was filled with hangings and ornaments that showed that this office was clearly run by a Native American chief. Two magnificent dream catchers hung from the ceiling, surrounding a bald eagle that had been carved out of wood. Native American textiles and animal masks decorated the walls,

---

[8] IBM, the IBM logo, and ibm.com® are trademarks or registered trademarks of International Business Machines Corp., registered in many jurisdictions worldwide.

and on top of the filing cabinet, there was a ceremonial sacred pipe seated on a carved piece of art.

Dr. Neale was a tall gentleman in his mid-sixties. Although he was wearing a business suit, instead of a tie, a silver Native ornament the size of a tennis ball hung from his neck. His salt-n-pepper hair was neatly arranged in two long, thick braids, which rested on his chest. "Come, please sit down," he said. From the moment we walked into his office, I felt like I was in Indian country. The energy of the moment prompted me to introduce myself with total transparency, free from the guarded mask I had learned to wear. "I am Ricardo Sánchez, a Native South American of Inka[9] descent," showing a side of myself that I rarely displayed to the world. He replied by speaking from his heart, saying, "I am Joe Raincrow Neale, and as Chief of the Yougiogaheny River Band of Shawnee Indians, I welcome you, brother Ricardo, to this ancient land we call Turtle Island (North America). The Eagle from the North welcomes the Condor from the South."

I felt a sudden chill, and I found myself on the verge of tears. My fear of being rejected completely vanished, and my heart was filled with a great sense of validation, acknowledgement, honor, and pride. His genuine greeting was a gift,

---

[9] The term **"Inka"** is derived from Quechua, the language of the Inca civilization, in which "Inka" means "governor" or "lord." The Spanish colonizers adapted many indigenous words to fit Spanish phonetic rules, which often altered spellings. In Spanish, the "k" sound was often replaced with a "c," which led to the term being written as **"Inca"** in colonial records and subsequent Western literature. Thus, "Inka" is increasingly favored, particularly in academic, historical, and cultural contexts in Peru, as it reflects the original Quechua form. Peru has experienced a resurgence in efforts to reclaim indigenous identity, languages, and cultural practices that were suppressed during and after the colonial period.

his way of performing a *Give Away*[10] ceremony. The moment I heard, "Condor from the South," it was as if my power animal and the Inka within were invoked. Instinctively, I pulled out the Andean wooden flute I always carried in my backpack, and I greeted him formally by playing a song that is dear to my heart, *El Condor Pasa,* composed by Daniel Alomía Robles.[11] That song was considered the instrumental hymn of the Andes. It is customary among most indigenous peoples in the Americas to greet one another by honoring the encounter of cultures and personal energy fields. And so, as an act of *Ayni*[12] (sacred reciprocity), I closed my eyes and played the flute, guided by the spirit of brotherhood and respect. What John and I had expected to be a business-like conversation was suddenly elevated to a sacred ceremony. On a higher dimension, Chief Neale's warmth and heartfelt welcome was the equivalent of a homecoming ceremony, in which he acknowledged my good intentions toward the new

---

[10] In some North Native American cultures, the "Give Away tradition is practiced during greetings or first-time meetings to show respect, hospitality, and goodwill. When meeting someone for the first time, individuals may offer a small gift as a gesture of friendship or to establish a positive relationship. This act symbolizes generosity and the importance of sharing within the community, fostering trust and mutual respect. The exchange reflects the deeply rooted cultural value of giving rather than taking.

[11] *El Condor Pasa* was written by Peruvian composer Daniel Alomía Robles in 1913. It gained international fame when Simon & Garfunkel adapted it in 1970, adding English lyrics to the traditional melody, popularizing it worldwide under the title, *El Condor Pasa (If I Could)*.

[12] *Ayni* is a sacred Andean tradition of reciprocity, rooted in mutual aid and interdependence. It embodies the principle of giving and receiving, where acts of kindness or labor are repaid in kind, fostering balance and harmony within communities and nature. *Ayni* reflects the deep Andean belief that everything is interconnected, and through this exchange, individuals maintain a flow of energy that nurtures all life.

land and its people and honored my journey. In so doing, he honored his Shawnee core principles. I, in return, gifted him a song from my heart, my transparent self, and my commitment to be a good student.

Chief Neale had served in the U.S. Navy during World War II (WWII). He was the principal chief of the Eagle clan, and he served as a spiritual leader of a band of several hundred members living in Maryland, Virginia, West Virginia, and Ohio. He was also an ordained Methodist minister as well as a lecturer on Indian affairs. After a short interchange, he said, "Education knows no borders; all you need is determination. I simply ask that you strive to be a diligent student. Welcome to American University!"

John had barely spoken this time, but he stood there next to me, seeing the fruits of his advocacy unfold. The cost of tuition was still an issue, but it was agreed that I could start by enrolling in one-credit classes until I could afford to pay the regular three-credit cost per class. On that magical day, the three of us—Chief Joe Raincrow Neale, Crazy Gringo John, and Condor Flute Boy—experienced an unforgettable moment that was both moving and healing. This life-changing event sparked in me a great interest to deepen my understanding of the Native American world view, cosmology, and struggles. Additionally, it planted the seed that would later allow me to explore the world of Native American healers[13] and the *paqos*[14] of the Americas.

---

[13] A Native American healer, or medicine man, is both a respected healer and spiritual guide. Their role is deeply rooted in tribal traditions and practices. They use herbal remedies, rituals, and prayers to heal and maintain harmony within their community.

[14] A **Paqo** is a spiritual practitioner of the Andean healing arts who help harmonize energies of individuals and their relations with their

John and I were both thrilled and grateful to Chief Neale for his decision, of course. Not just because I'd been admitted to AU, but also because we were experiencing a powerful testament of our cross-cultural friendship in real time. We truly felt that my admission to AU was the result of our collaborative friendship beyond borders. Can you imagine if everyone treated each other in the same manner? What if, instead of feeding fear and separation, people instead took off their armor, showed their true selves, and lived in harmony, as the Creator intended? Inspired by our triumph and the possibilities contained within these questions, John and I went home and created an imaginary world we called, "Amigos America."

By the end of that year, Chief Neale retired from American University with honors. However, he continued working in his role as chief of the Yougiogaheny River Band of Shawnee Indians until he made his journey to the spirit world in 1998.

Amigos America

Amigos America was inspired by both Shawnee Chief Raincrow Neale's welcoming ceremony at American University and the friendship between John and I. It celebrates unique friendships and recognizes that although people may come from different worlds with different life challenges, we

---

communities. They maintain a deep, reciprocal relationship with the Cosmos, Pachamama (Mother Earth), the Apus (mountain spirits), and nature's living energies. Paqos serve their communities through the Andean principle of ayni (reciprocity), helping balance energies rather than seeking personal power or isolation.

may still share deep longings. In our case, focusing on our commonalities instead of our differences enabled us to heal from our very different past experiences as we enjoyed and learned from each other's cultures, jokes, and perspectives. Amigos America became our private "club." When blessing our meals or toasting each other over a beer, we often included a special toast for Amigos America, to celebrate our brotherhood, mutual respect, and care that surpassed our racial and cultural differences.

Amigos America had a societal or "public" component embedded in the power differential between us. As a white, middle-aged man, John had certain privileges that I, as a young, undocumented Latino immigrant, did not. Because of his keen awareness of his rights as an American citizen, John never hesitated to defend those rights if they were violated. He also always defended others' rights, too, including mine, when needed.

To honor its meaning and importance, I created an Amigos America logo—a bright yellow sun with wavy thick sun-rays emanating across a blue background, representing the light and love that friendships bring and the many ways we can reach out to help each other. John turned the logo into a flag and hung it on the apartment wall, where we lived together as roommates. We took the flag to Latino festivals in Washington, D.C. and waved it proudly. On picnics with immigrant friends, we always made sure it was prominently displayed. Some people thought we were naïve when we explained its meaning—after all, how many grownups "play" in fantasy worlds where people live in a society free of segregationist ideas and behaviors, where no one belief, race, color, faith, or nationality are better than another, where everyone belongs and feels at home? Once we pointed out that Amigos America is no different from what every religion, fraternity/sorority, and sacred scripture teaches, some of them started to understand. Our collective problem is that we tend to disconnect from these teachings in the day-to-day world, we often explained. Amigos America is a call to our collective conscience to help bring back the American spirit of belonging to our neighborhoods, schools, colleges, workplaces, and places of worship.

Amigos America honors Chief Neale and John, both of whom are now in the spirit world. They may not have been famous, but their teachings and deeds on this planet changed the lives of many people living in the shadows. They knew the secret of life: treat each other with respect, make your relatives feel at home, and consider the future impact of your decisions.

Photo 4. Posing for a photo at my dishwashing station in the Spring of 1987 at a prominent hotel in Washington, D.C.

CHAPTER 4

America the Difficult

"Do not oppress a foreigner; you yourselves know how it feels to be foreigners, because you were foreigners in Egypt."

~ Exodus 23:9

I dreamt of being able to work without the constant fear of deportation looming over me. With a legal work permit, my life would take a remarkable turn. I could buy a car, secure a comfortable apartment, even start my own business. I could truly chase the American Dream. I desired it with such intensity that I could almost taste it.

One afternoon in the Summer of 1987, a Central American coworker shared that he was the recipient of a legal work permit. He had gotten it from the Immigration and Naturalization Service (INS) after filing a petition for political asylum. At the time, migration from El Salvador, Honduras, and Guatemala was heavy due to the civil wars that had scourged most of the region. The Reagan administration had reluctantly agreed to grant limited protective status to certain Central American immigrants who could prove that their lives would be in danger if they returned to Central America. Many immigrants quietly rushed to hire immigration lawyers or paralegals to file the required documents. An immigrant visa was not guaranteed, but at least the applicants could apply for renewable legal work permits.

My roommate and I talked about the political turmoil in Peru and how unsafe it was to be in certain regions of the country. Peru was heading toward civil war, just like in Central America. "What if we submit a request for a work permit based on the political instability in Peru? Do you think we'd have a chance?" he said. The idea was both exciting and terrifying. If we risked it, the immigration authorities would get our information and could use it to detain or deport us if we didn't qualify. After weighing all our options, we decided to go ahead and pursue the petition. *"Que sea lo que Dios quiera,"* I finally said. Let's leave it in the hands of God.

We couldn't afford a lawyer, so we hired a middle-age Salvadoran paralegal who specialized in helping people get legal work permits so they could escape the traumas of war. He said, "There is a small window of time for Central Americans to apply for political asylum work permits, but South Americans are having a harder time getting temporary protection because no civil wars are happening there, at least not yet. We can still submit a petition, though. At least you may qualify for a temporary work permit while the asylum petition is in progress," he added. It was a huge gamble, not to mention very expensive. We each had to pay a $500 nonrefundable fee for the paralegal's advice and services. He told us to gather documentation, including our job histories, and information to build our cases, such as newspaper articles about the deteriorating and unsafe situation in Peru. When my packet was ready, I took a deep breath and began an anxiety-filled trip to the INS office for my 8 am appointment. During the Metro ride, my PTSD symptoms started kicking in—my palms were sweating, and flashbacks of the helicopter came to mind. I tried to slow my way-too-fast heartbeat, but it was hard because I was hyperalert, in fight or flight mode.

In the soulless waiting room, dozens of Central Americans were sitting on hard gray chairs, waiting for their names to be called. Some paced back and forth, trying to calm their anxiety with constant movement. The quiet, tense energy in the waiting room reminded me of the U.S. Embassy in Lima and my attempts to get a tourist visa. Again, I saw people praying, trying to connect with a higher power and asking for help and good results. My prayers were repeatedly interrupted by crazy thoughts about INS law enforcement officers storming the building, rounding us up, and deporting us all at once.

A voice from behind the counter interrupted my catastrophizing, calling out, "Ricardo Sánchez, window number four!" I stood up with my heart trembling and walked toward the window, silently repeating, *"Creator, it's all in your hands. It is all in your hands."* I handed my folder to the officer at the window. The officer scanned my documents and forms, asked a couple of questions, wrote something on one of the forms, and handed me an Alien Card[1]. (Yes, there

---

[1] The Arrival/Departure Record I-94 form known by the immigrant community as the "Alien Card" was a paper form issued to non-U.S. citizens upon entry into the United States. This card was provided by the

really is such a thing. An Alien Card is an ID card for "extraterrestrials" like me.) I was beyond thrilled—the card granted me a permit to work for one whole year! As weird as it may sound, I felt immensely proud of my new status as an official alien because that new Alien Card temporarily allowed me to work legally in the U.S., my planet Earth, so to speak. The INS officer told me that I should receive a decision about my asylum petition in about ten months.

I soared home on wings of euphoria, grateful for the temporary respite from the shadows of fear. With my legal work permit in hand, I wasted no time in strengthening my work status at the temp agency. I stopped by to give them a copy of my new legal document in the hopes that they would book me at better paying jobs instead of the usual dishwashing jobs. With such a productive morning at the INS office and the temp agency, I went home feeling unstoppable, because I'd made huge progress toward achieving my dreams in America.

I arrived at my apartment and took my laundry bag to the communal washers in the basement of the building and left the machine running while I went to eat lunch before heading to work. A few minutes into my lunch, I put my hand in my left shirt pocket to take another look at my "golden" Alien Card. My euphoria quickly morphed into panic, again. It wasn't there! I checked all my other pockets and nothing. It wasn't in my wallet, either. *Shit! Where was it?* Then, I

Immigration and Naturalization Service prior to creation of the Department of Homeland Security in 2003. Travelers would receive a physical card that was stapled into their passport, which they had to keep until their departure. This card was also provided to people already in the U.S. as the first step to regularize their immigration status, whether as asylum seekers or under temporary protection status.

remembered that I had put it in the left pocket of a shirt that was now inside the washing machine!

I ran down the two flights of stairs to the basement at top speed, desperate to stop the washer. Desperately pulling the dripping wet yellow shirt out of the machine, I realized that all that was left of the Alien Card was a little wet paper ball. Carefully, I tried to unfold the wet blob, but it disintegrated even more. The ink had been washed out. It was completely gone. I was simultaneously in a panic and furious at myself. *How could I be so stupid?! That piece of paper was my life! There's no way that the INS would give me another copy*, I thought. *I would probably have to pay again.* Just as I was about to collapse into tears, I remembered that I had given the temp agency a copy of my Alien Card. I quickly finished my laundry and headed back to the agency to ask for a copy of my "golden" document. I don't think it's an exaggeration to say that holding that photocopy was the only thing that kept me sane that day.

A few days later, I applied for a social security number and acquired a photo ID. I waited anxiously for them to arrive in the mail, and just when they did, I was laid off from the temp agency. D.C.'s hospitality industry is virtually dead during the summer, so there was little need for temporary workers like me. The hot weather in the city meant that fewer businesses chose to hold conventions in the city's hotels, opting instead for convention centers close to the ocean.

Back to zero cash and no work, I had to figure out another way to pay my bills. Even though I had been paying taxes from the start, I hadn't been in the system long enough to qualify for unemployment benefits. To survive, I started looking for occasional day-labor jobs in between my English classes. One afternoon while waiting for the bus, I noticed an elderly lady pushing a little two-wheel grocery cart walking toward me. She stopped at the bus stop, and I quickly stood up to give her my seat, a habit I had learned in childhood. She thanked me and took the seat. As we waited for the bus together, she looked at me and asked, "Where are you from?" With a smile, I responded that I was from Peru. "How long have you been here?" She asked, this time in Spanish. "About seven months," I responded. It was clear from her accent that she wasn't from the U.S., so I asked her the same question. It turned out that she was from Cuzco, Peru and had migrated to the U.S. during the Carter administration. Then she asked, "Where do you work?" I told her that I had been laid off and was looking for work. I asked if she needed any work done at her home, hoping she might hire me for a day or two. Ignoring my question, she said, "My daughter works at the World Bank, and she mentioned that they have an opening. It's for a clerical position." The bus arrived and interrupted our conversation, but I followed her down the aisle and sat next to her, hoping she would tell me more about the job. She said that it was an entry-level position, and it involved sorting library books and filing. Then she asked, "Are you interested in the job?" "Of course!" I said. She promised to find out more details, adding that she planned to see her daughter later that day. We exchanged phone numbers, and before I got off the bus, she said, "My daughter has two German Shepherds, and she has to go out of town for a week. Would you be interested in taking care of the dogs? She will pay you." Again, I said, "Of course!"

Saying yes to every respectable job opportunity was my mantra back in those days. I believed that this woman was an angel sent by God to assist me, and I started to dream once more. The World Bank, wow! It was unbelievable that I might get to work at the most powerful financial institution in the world! I had heard so much about the influence of that institution, and I was both thrilled and scared about the prospect of working there.

A few days later, I met the lady's daughter for lunch at the World Bank's cafeteria, and she filled me in on the details of the position. She was a young Peruvian American who had been brought to the U.S. as a child. At the World Bank, she oversaw the Latin American section of the library. She asked for a copy of my resume, and I was glad that I had thought far enough ahead to polish it (with a little help from my roommates, Franco and John). Thanks to my new connection, I was granted an interview a week later that included a filing test. The interview went well, and I couldn't have been happier when I answered the phone a few days later and heard, "Mr. Sánchez, you are hired! We want you to start work this coming Monday."

Who would have thought that such a dramatic "career" change was even possible? Just three weeks before, I had been working as a dishwasher in humid, greasy basements, sweating and scrubbing endless piles of pots and pans. Now, I wore business suits, had my own desk and phone, and worked on an IBM computer. It was surreal! I kept pinching myself to make sure it wasn't a dream. My salary jumped from $3.35 to $7.00 per hour. After a 3-month probationary term working through a temp agency, I became a direct World Bank employee around Christmas of 1987. I also worked at different hotels on the weekends—the temporary service had rehired me a few months back, when business had picked up again—mainly at banquets on an on-call basis.

Having a work permit made a world of difference; it provided a huge psychological boost. I felt less like a peasant and more like a human. It gave me more confidence to walk around with less fear. My work permit was not just a document; to me, it was the source of immense hope. It allowed me to dream again. Although I was still alone in the U.S., my spirits were high, and I lowered my guard a bit and was less hypersensitive about being detained or deported. It was as if a heavy load had been lifted off my shoulders. The renewed self-confidence helped bring my outgoing personality back; and I was even better able to express myself in English.

Latin Lover Blues

On weekends, I often spent time browsing the newsstand at Editorial El Mundo, a Latino bookstore in *El Barrio Latino*, D.C.'s Latin district, which stocked Peruvian magazines and newspapers. I skimmed through the latest news from Peru, which was typically 3-4 weeks old by the time it got to D.C. Most of the news from Peru was depressing. The front pages of the newspapers were filled with stories on the collapsing economy and deadly attacks by Shining Path guerillas or the Peruvian Army. Sometimes, I bought music or Spanish-language self-help books on cassette tapes. Over time, that small bookstore became my favorite place to hang out on Saturday afternoons.

One day, while browsing the newspapers, I lifted my head, turned around, and noticed a beautiful brunette white girl about my age working at the counter in the back of store where the baptismal and *quinceañera* birthday party ornaments were sold. I said to myself, *wow, what is this mamacita doing here?* We made eye contact from across the store. *Mama mia! She is looking at me! Come on, go talk to her!* I coached myself. But what could I say? *How about, Hi?! But then what? Shit! I don't know what to say! Just go, maybe she speaks Spanish*, I kept talking to myself. Then, I remembered my days back in Peru, when I would bravely go up to girls clear across the room and ask them to dance. *Come on, boy, you can do this!*

I walked surreptitiously toward her while browsing the merchandise in her section, which I had no intention of buying. My heart was beating faster as I got closer. "Hi!" I said with a smile. She reciprocated with an angelic smile. *So far, so good*, I thought. *Now what? Shit! Either keep speaking or turn around and go back to the bookshelf in the corner. Continue!* A little voice commanded me. It was my first time trying to flirt in broken English. I may have been sweating and nervous on the inside, but I was careful to look like a cool Latin lover on the outside. I asked, "Do you speak Spanish, *señorita*?" "*Un poquito*," she replied with the cutest smile. We flirted for a few more minutes in Spanglish or Engliñol, I'm not sure which.

Her name was Donna, and like me, she was 19 years old. Even though we'd exchanged only a few words, to me, it felt like love at first sight. Every weekend, I looked forward to the chance to talk to her. I took the bus across town just to buy a piece of candy at the store where she worked so I could chat with her and casually browse the news, all the while looking at her from behind the newspapers I was pretending to read. Donna was the second of two siblings. She had grown up in New York, but when her parents divorced a few years before, she decided to move to Washington, D.C. to distance herself from the family drama. She was independent and beautiful.

Donna and I dated for a few weeks, and each time we went out together, I fell more in love with her. One day, I took Donna out to dance at a salsa club in Georgetown. After a fun night of dancing, I recited to her what I had been practicing in front of my mirror for days, "Donna, I had a great time hanging out with you these past few weeks, and quite honestly my feelings for you are, are…" My English vocabulary was reaching its max, and my throat felt jammed with all the words and thoughts I wanted to say beautifully in English. *Yes, you can do it, Latin lover! Just say it, man!* The little voice inside kept repeating. Meanwhile, Donna was patiently waiting for me to finish the sentence. "Donna, I… [swallowing the rock in my throat], I love you."

She looked at me with the most lovely and tender face and smiled. With the palm of her hand, she stroked my left cheek, and we kissed. My heart went from beating anxiously in my chest to beating with joy and rejuvenation. "Donna, I want to be your boyfriend, would you give me that honor?" In her flirty style, she told me that she would think about it and give me her answer in two weeks. I was convinced that she was as crazy in love with me as I was with her. "Ok," I responded, undeterred. I was already dreaming of Donna as my girlfriend and then, my fiancé. *Not only did I have a successful career at the World Bank*, I thought, *but now I can share my American Dream with Donna!*

It wasn't long before I discovered that my exuberance had been premature. Just as I was starting to feel a sense of order in my life, not one but two events knocked me down in the same week, like the classic one-two punch. First, Donna said "no" to my request to be her boyfriend, claiming that she was moving to another state and wasn't ready for a love commitment. Second, a letter arrived from the INS office. With an already broken heart, I read the letter:

> Mr. Sánchez, your political asylum petition has been denied. Peru's situation at the moment is not considered critical, and the Department of Justice is not granting political protection except in extreme cases. You have 30 days from the date of this letter to leave the United States. Failure to leave the country within the specified time will result in your imminent detention and deportation. Being deported will ban you from applying for any type of visa in the future.

I froze, not sure what to do. I felt like my world was crumbling and a dusty, dark storm was coming my way. The days that followed were filled with denial, anger, fear, and confusion. I quit my promising job at the World Bank, moved to another place, and abruptly stopped all my routines, terrified at the idea of being hunt down, incarcerated, and deported. I went back to living in the shadows.

Teachings from the Shadows

My days in America were coming to an end, and I needed to change and adapt to make the most of the days that remained. Aware of my new reality, I needed to keep my costs down and save as much money as possible. I searched for a low-rent room and found a place for $50 dollars a month in a basement in the heart of Washington D.C.'s Latino district, known in English as Mount Pleasant. The price was too good to be true, so I went to check the place out.

From the outside, it looked like a traditional house, built over a century ago as part of a public housing project. It was owned by a Guatemalan couple. The owner said that the room in the basement was still available, so I paid one month's rent in advance and moved in the following day. I only had two small cardboard boxes and two backpacks filled with clothes. My room was one of seven tiny divisions that the owner had made in the basement. Calling them "rooms" was a real stretch. They were more like jail cells; except they were separated by plywood instead of bars. One 25-watt incandescent lightbulb hung from the ceiling of each room, so I literally lived in the shadows. The back wall of my space was a real wall made of drywall with studs. The only problem was that there was a hole about the size of a soccer ball at the base of the wall, which I covered with one of my cardboard boxes. All the basement tenants shared a single, small common shower, toilet, and sink, which were in the corner of the dark, cold basement. The plywood dividers provided no privacy from the tenants living "next door." The first and second floors were also divided into one-person studios. Some of the tenants were single immigrants, but a few families with small children were also squeezed into a few of the studios. In all, at least 18 people lived in the 3-story house. I soon understood why the rent was too good to be true. The hole in the wall of my room had been created by the rats that ran through the walls of the house all night long. It was hard to sleep, because all night long I could hear the rats running between the ceiling and the walls.

Some of the loudest noise came not from the rats but from my human neighbors, especially a Honduran female tenant. Her name was Mariela, and she had a "freelance" business in the evenings, providing "services" to up to three men per night between 7 pm and 2 am. She was a sex worker, and because of the nature of her business, she kept a low profile in the house. My Catholic upbringing had taught me that prostitutes were evil creatures who were destined to burn in hell for their sins, so I was surprised to discover that Mariela was a nice, otherwise normal Central American lady. Her day job was to cook meals for some of the other tenants in the house. She stored the meals in labeled lunch boxes in the refrigerator and sold them to tenants who did not have the time or know-how to cook for themselves. Because we shared the common kitchen table and used the same bathroom facilities, Mariela and I began to chat occasionally. We shared our immigrant stories and exchanged anecdotes about our experiences in our new country. She was a single mother, and she had two children, ages 4 and 6, who were under the care of her mother in Honduras. She showed me photos of her children and told me how much she missed them. She had not seen them since coming to America 3 years prior, and the separation was tearing her apart.

Although I liked Mariela as a person and empathized with her struggles, my feelings toward her were conflicted. How was it possible that this "evil woman," who, according to my Catholic upbringing, was going to hell, could be such a decent human being and loving mother? There were so many questions I wanted to ask about her night business. *Aren't you afraid of these men? Do you know them? What if you get caught?* But I knew that I didn't have the right to ask those question, and even if I did, I didn't know how. Somehow, Mariela sensed my inner angst and desire to know more about her. One day, she said, "Come here, Ricardo, have a seat over here," gesturing toward the foot of her narrow bed. "What would you like to know?" She was relaxed, sitting on her bed with a tiny radio on low volume. As I started walking towards her bed, a flood of thoughts passed through my mind, mainly scenes from *The Exorcist* and similar horror movies. Then, I suddenly realized that I had allowed fears inflicted by Hollywood and my Catholic upbringing to demonize this lady, an immigrant mom and human being who was doing her best to survive and help her children. As I sat on her bed, I realized I had just crossed another border. We had a respectful conversation, exchanged jokes, and she answered my questions with admirable frankness and honesty. It was ok. I felt I had just gotten to know an incredible human being, a loving and resilient mom.

The basement lacked chairs for sitting or reading and it was too loud for napping, despite lacking a TV. I generally only used it for crashing at night. I began leaving early to go to work, usually around 6 am, and didn't come back until late at night. The house was infested not only with rats but also cockroaches; we were obviously living in a place that violated just about every healthy living standard. I wondered if the inspectors knew about those kinds of houses. The owner only came to the house once or twice a month, and only then, to collect rent payments. It was the worst place I had ever stayed, but I could not report the living conditions for fear of being caught by immigration agents and deported. In fact, I changed my life drastically to avoid being detained or deported by them, including disconnecting from most of my friends and avoiding the places where I used to hang out. The only thing I didn't change was my class at American University. But I read and did homework at local libraries, never in my cockroach and rat-infested room.

Eventually, I'd had enough of the horrible living conditions in the basement, so I screwed up my courage and began looking for a new place to live. After a few days, I found a room in an apartment in Arlington, Virginia. I packed all my belongings in the trunk of a taxicab and moved to the immigrant neighborhood known as "Little Vietnam." True to its name, the area was home to many Vietnamese immigrants and refugees who had escaped from conflict during and after the Vietnam war, which had ended in 1975. I moved into the apartment of a young immigrant couple. Gloria was from Peru and Toni—his American name—was from Vietnam. Both spoke terrible English, but they were terrific, caring human beings. Their home was peaceful, loving, and warm. They had a little boy whose main job was to run around the house all day and act as the family translator, when needed. They treated me like a member of the family and invited me to gatherings of their family and Vietnamese friends in the building and around the neighborhood. I felt welcomed and loved by everyone. Although my commute to and from D.C. was longer, it was well worth it.

Moving into my new home in Arlington felt like the beginning of a new era. Although at $200 per month, the rent was expensive (from my standpoint, that is), it brought much needed peace of mind. At least it was one less basic need to worry about, which was key because I still had so many others left to attend to. After all, the length of my stay in the U.S. was anything but certain, due to my immigration status, so I tried to prepare myself mentally for whatever lay ahead. I decided to work and save money for two years or until immigration deported me, whichever came first. My new goal was to find the best job I could get in my current circumstance, work my butt off, and live each day as if it were my last day in America, which it very well may have been.

Creator, Please Give Me a Second Chance

The better home environment in Arlington, Virginia lifted my spirits. That helped to heighten my determination to do my best in my remaining time in America, which fed my cautious search for job opportunities. Before long, an intriguing position in the local Spanish newspaper caught my eye. "*El Latino Newspaper* is looking for an enthusiastic person to assist the production team," the ad read, "no previous experience needed." Longing to go back to working in an office environment, I decided to go check it out. I made an appointment for an interview, and to my pleasant surprise, the director of the newspaper was Peruvian. She was a very busy but nice lady who, together with her husband, had been running the newspaper for about 10 years.

In the interview, I found out that the job of a "production assistant" included cleaning the office four days a week and helping the truck driver deliver the newspapers to Latino businesses around the D.C. metropolitan area (also known as the DMV—D.C., Maryland, and Virginia) on Fridays. While the ad didn't outright lie, it cleverly gave the illusion that the job was an office position. Even though it felt like a "gotcha" ad to me, there was something about the energy of the lady and the employees' good humor that was attractive nonetheless. And then there was the fact that they didn't ask me for documents. I decided to take the job, even though the starting salary was just $6.00 per hour.

The newspaper was located in Adams Morgan, a traditional neighborhood in Northwest Washington, D.C. The newspaper's small office was on the second and third floors of a three-level, rundown townhouse built at the turn of the 20th century. The weekly newspaper was available to the public for free, which meant that it relied solely on advertising sales to stay in business. *El Latino* was rich in socio/community capital, but it struggled financially. The paper was considered "the" voice of the growing Latino immigrant community in Washington, D.C. Not surprisingly, the production team was overworked and underpaid. In addition to cleaning the office, I was soon given other tasks, including running errands, making coffee for the staff, and moving the cars of employees, who had a hard time finding parking for more than two hours, due to the limited number of parking spaces in the neighborhood.

Soon after I was hired, the newspaper was sold to a Central American businessman whose main business was in real estate. He bought the newspaper to diversify his investment portfolio. After the purchase, he hired a bottom-line driven director, Mr. Fariz, who restructured the management team in an attempt to turn the paper into a profitable business.

In 1989, producing a newspaper was a labor-intensive process. First, newspaper articles had to be typed and printed out. Then, each news item had to be carefully cut out and manually coated with wax on the back. The coated news items were then pasted onto large cardboard sheets, which served as templates for the printer. The entire process had to be completed from start to finish every Thursday night. That same night, the set of templates, known as the 'master' dummy sheet, had to be delivered physically to the printing press, located 25 miles away in Maryland. Under the new management, no one was allowed to leave the office until the master dummy sheet had been sent to the printers. This often meant that the entire crew had to stay at work until the wee hours on Friday morning.

One day, Marcos, the editor-in-chief, asked if I could help type up news articles on the new Apple MacIntosh® computer[2] (scanners had not yet been invented). I enthusiastically said, "Of course!" I had always wanted to use a Mac, which was known for its revolutionary new technology, the "mouse." The World Bank had only used IBM computers, which ran on the Microsoft operating systems. I had heard that Macs were easy to use, and you didn't need to have any programming skills to use them.

Marcos was pleased with my work. Not only did he keep giving me articles to type, but he also asked me to help transcribe audiotaped interviews that the reporters had conducted during the week. Gradually, I spent more time typing, which meant less cleaning. Within two months, I was promoted to a "real" production assistant position, and my boss asked if I had a driver's license. He said that he wanted me to drive the new pickup truck on a new, expanded delivery

---

[2] Macintosh® is a registered trademark of Apple Inc. The Macintosh, introduced by Apple in 1984, was the first personal computer to feature a graphical user interface and a mouse, revolutionizing user-friendly computing. It debuted with a famous Super Bowl ad and became a foundation for modern Apple products.

route. I told him that I knew how to drive but needed a couple weeks to get my license. With my Peruvian passport, a letter from my employer, and my social security card, I was able to apply for a driver's license, and within days, I was the proud owner of my own driver license. The cleaning position was given to a Honduran high school student, who was also new in the country.

One day, I volunteered to draw cartoons—one of my hidden talents—for the editorial page. Marcos loved that idea and readily accepted my offer. A few months later, I was promoted again. This time, I became the manager of the classified ad section and put in charge of ad sales and creating content for that section. As much as the owners loved my go-getter attitude and artistic talent, what they loved even more was that I was willing to work so enthusiastically for such a small paycheck. I knew that my speedy promotion and accomplishments at the newspaper could end at any time, however, because of my legal situation. I was afraid the new owner would find out I was undocumented and fire me. Plus, I feared being detained and deported by "La Migra," which could happen anytime, anywhere. Rather than let fear consume me, I decided to take a risk and tell Mr. Fariz the truth about my legal status.

I pulled him aside one day when he was in a good mood, explained my legal situation, and asked him to sponsor me to obtain a work visa. To my relief, he responded positively, and within a few weeks, he signed and submitted the paperwork to the INS office. Although the wait time ranged between 3-6 years, this step gave me hope that I might finally be able to become legal in the U.S., or at least receive a legal work permit while the paperwork was considered. On my

21ˢᵗ birthday, I updated my birthday wish to: *"Creator, please allow me to stay legally in America."*

Photo 5. Playing the guitar with the choir at Our Lady of the Americas Catholic Church in Washington, D.C. in the Summer of 1987.

Photo 6. Sharing some Andean music with my art classmates at the end of the Fall semester at American University in 1987.

CHAPTER 5

Two Worlds Unite

"I love you not for who you are,
but for who I am when I am with you."

~ Gabriel García Márquez

One day on a chilly January morning, when I was typing a news story, the Creator responded to my birthday wish by sending me a female angel. She sat next to me to assist with additional typing jobs. The angel introduced herself: *"Hola,* my name is Kathy, I am the new Washington Metropolitan reporter-in-training, also known as the new intern." She had blue eyes, an innocent smile, a shy personality, and she spoke Spanish with a strange accent, part-gringo, part-Spanish from Spain... I loved everything about her. I thought to myself, *The Creator must be undocumented, He knows what I am going through. He knows about the unifying power of love.*

I started looking forward to work on the days that "my" favorite reporter came to the office. She, too, was studying at American University, and the job at *El Latino* was part of her internship program requirements. She had come from Chicago to pursue a degree in international relations and Spanish. During her junior year in college, she had participated in a 10-month cultural exchange program in Spain, where she had acquired a funny accent from Seville. I, on the other hand, still spoke very bumpy English, which I'd learned through my art class at AU and my full-time, hands-on "immersion program" on the streets of America.

The language barrier did not stop us from falling in love in front of "our" Macintosh computers, where we eagerly corrected each other's transcriptions and clarified ambiguous translations. Our eyes, smiles, and gestures helped us communicate better than our spoken words. Our productivity and the quality of our work went up, too, I bet. Our hearts were excited and joyful, and everything felt right. Having lunch together at work soon turned into dating, weekends together, and occasional nights out at local Latin night clubs. I met Kathy's parents, her younger sister, and her paternal grandmother a few months after she joined the newspaper, when they came to D.C. for her college graduation. They were super nice, and I was very shy and hyperaware of our cultural and racial differences. I didn't want to say or do anything that may make me look awkward or give a bad first impression.

On one of our dates, I had to be honest with Kathy and tell her about my legal situation before we committed to a serious relationship. Not knowing what her reaction would be, I said, "I am undocumented, and my future in the U.S. is uncertain. I plan to stay here another 15 months and will then leave the country before I am kicked out." I paused, and an awkward silence invaded the park bench where we were sitting. "Would you come visit me in Peru if it comes to that?" I said, breaking the silence. "Are you crazy? I will go with you," she responded. Out from the caves of my subconscious mind, a thought surfaced that was probably heavily influenced by my traditional Catholic upbringing. *You can't live with someone from the opposite sex unless you marry her.* At that moment, my faith and current legal status created an unusual pressure within me. The elephant in the room needed to be faced, regardless of the outcome, and with a sudden burst of courage, I said, "Kathy, would you... I mean... would you... what if... we got married?" The words felt as if they were jammed in my throat, like my heart and mind needed more time to process them. I then completed my sentence by saying "...that way, we could move to Peru?"

Kathy was caught completely off guard by my request. She understood that circumstances could change in the future, but she had never anticipated having to make such a significant decision on that particular day. We were both just 21, after all, and the topic of marriage had not been on either of our radars. I had thought about it previously as a remote possibility, but never as a high probability. There were no easy answers to questions as big as that one. "Give me a day to think about it, and I will give you an answer tomorrow," she finally said.

I went home and spent the entire night pondering our conversation. I knew I wanted to be with Kathy, but our situation was complex. On a personal level, our relationship brought me joy, but the uncertainty of my legal status and the potential complications it posed for our relationship left me feeling anxious and unsure about what lay ahead. I woke up the next day with the timid sunrays warming my face softly, as if telling me, *it's ok. There is no need to be anxious. Your heart is in the right place.* I felt a sense of peace, as if no matter what happened that day, everything would be ok.

Kathy and I met at our favorite restaurant in *El Barrio Latino*. We looked at each other, smiled, and as I got closer, my eyes got bigger, ready to listen her heart speak. "Yes!" she said, simply, and something beautiful inflated our beings. We kissed while tears ran down our faces. We were thrilled and in awe at having made the biggest decision of our lives together, in complete autonomy, a decision that felt right for the two of us.

Now what? We wondered, in search of a place to land after our short trip to the clouds. Both of our families came to mind. "Should we tell them now or get married first and tell them later?" we asked each other. It was a difficult question because we both loved our parents and wanted to share our plans. However, due to the circumstances, we decided to skip all the formalities—the ceremonies, church stuff, and parental blessings. Time was of the essence, and even though we hated having to hide this important decision and seminal life event from everyone we knew—even our own families—we felt like doing so was necessary to move the process along as quickly as possible.

Three months later, on a hot summer day, we got married in a simple but love-filled ceremony at the D.C. courthouse. On the day of our appointment at the courthouse's Office of Marriage Licenses, we took a taxi to the courthouse but went to the wrong office building. We spent about 15 minutes looking for the office. "It is 8:00 o'clock, we don't want to miss our wedding!" I said, holding Kathy's hand as we ran through the hallways and stairways. When we finally arrived, the deputy clerk noticed we were breathing hard. She smiled and said, "Here you are! I knew you guys wouldn't miss this appointment!" After a short preamble aimed at making sure we knew what we were getting into, she married us at 8:20 am, and by 8:30 am, I was off to work at the newspaper office. Kathy stayed and went next door to the federal courthouse because her work assignment at that time was to report on the trial of the (then-current) Washington, D.C. Mayor Marion Barry.[1]

It took a few weeks until we finally got up the courage to break the news to our parents. Kathy's parents were more surprised than mine. They hadn't known the details of my immigration status, so it took some explaining. My parents were also caught by surprise even though they obviously were aware of my legal situation. Thankfully, both sets of parents gave us their blessing once they had assimilated the news. In retrospect, we couldn't be more grateful to our parents for recovering so quickly from the shocking news we'd so suddenly sprung on them. Somehow, they had managed to support us anyway, even though they surely must have had their own private doubts and concerns about our abrupt union. The fact that they found it in their hearts to do this spoke volumes about the depth of their love for us.

We moved into a small apartment in a predominantly immigrant neighborhood in Arlington, Virginia, located about

---

[1] Marion Barry was a four-term mayor of Washington, D.C., serving from 1979 to 1991 and from 1995 to 1999. Known as a civil rights activist, he played a significant role in shaping the city's political landscape, despite controversy during his career, including a 1990 arrest for drug charges.

a mile away from "Little Vietnam." Luckily, we were able to use the old car I had bought for $300 to help us move before it died just two days later. Even more luckily, the seller agreed to take it back when I told him how quickly it had broken down! Mr. Fariz also let us use the newspaper van to move our mattress, clothes, and books after I'd finished my Friday newspaper distribution route. We both were earning very modest salaries at the newspaper, so hiring a moving service was out of the question. Our worldly belongings were so few, however, that it only took one trip. Over time, we gradually bought two chairs, a small table, and a few pans and plates from a local thrift store, as our income allowed.

The manager at the newspaper where we both worked, Mr. Fariz had a mercurial nature. In the community, he was a public relations pro who knew how to schmooze the business community and politicians. But his employees got to see both sides of his personality. Some days, he was high energy and generous; other days, his arrogant, overbearing side took center stage. I think he got edgy because he was under so much pressure to make the newspaper break even. I felt bad for him, of course, but I couldn't stomach the way he sometimes used his position of authority to cross boundaries with undocumented employees, myself included, and others who he knew would not complain. Tired of the mistreatment and miserly salary, I left the newspaper three months after Kathy and I got married. A few weeks later, the newspaper started laying off employees, including Kathy.

The economic recession of 1991 soon put an end to *El Latino*, which closed its doors a few months after we had both left; and many small and medium businesses struggled to stay solvent. For most of the next year, Kathy and I struggled to make ends meet. After weeks of searching, I finally found a part-time job at a t-shirt screen printing place. Kathy worked on and off as a temporary secretary at various office buildings; but sometimes, a week or more would go by when the phone wouldn't ring.

One day, our luck finally began to change when Kathy got a phone call from the temp agency asking if she could fill in for a secretary at an international organization who'd suddenly returned to her home country in Latin America to tend to an ailing family member. They would need her for at least three months, the temp agency said, much to our relief. The temp assignment didn't pay much, however, so she also got a part-time job as a salesperson in a store at the mall in the evening and on the weekends. Meanwhile, I slowly started finding more frequent work as a freelance graphic design artist. Finally, we had enough income to pay our rent and buy groceries, too! It's a good thing we began getting steadier paychecks because as it turned out, we needed extra money not just to pay for the basics but to buy airplane tickets. Less than a year after we were married, a letter arrived in the mail from the Immigration and Naturalization Service asking me to go back to Peru.

Go Back to Peru!

"Mr. Sánchez, the interview for your resident visa will be in 30 days. You must return to Lima for your interview at the U.S. Embassy." I was thrilled to receive the letter, but the last sentence scared me. It reminded me of all the stories I had heard about people going back to get their papers who never returned, due to complications. Kathy and I knew that if they denied me a visa, it would affect not just me, but our marriage, as well. We decided not to take any chances. We would travel together. Regardless of the outcome, we pledged to stay together. And so, we gathered all the INS required documentation and traveled to Peru in May of 1991.

It was Kathy's first time in a so-called "third world country."[2] She had reasons to be scared, too. Peru was in a downward economic spiral, and the crime rate in Lima was very high, largely due to terrorist and drug-related violence. Lima was the target of almost daily violent campaigns by the insurgent movements against the government and civilians leading to widespread instability and violence.[3]

When we arrived in Lima, we stayed at the home of a colleague we had met at *El Latino*. Our colleague's mother and sister graciously welcomed us into their home, which was about an hour's drive from the U.S. Embassy. We arrived five days before my appointment at the Embassy because we needed to gather additional crucial documentation.

---

[2] The term "third-world country" originated during the Cold War to describe nations unaligned with the U.S. or Soviet Union but later became associated with poverty and underdevelopment. Today, it is considered outdated and often replaced by more respectful terms like "developing country," "Global South," or classifications like "low-income" or "lower-middle-income" countries. These modern terms emphasize economic status and potential for growth rather than a static condition of disadvantage.

[3] A 1992 Amnesty International report titled, Peru: Eight Years of Disappearances, states on p. 2: "According to the Senate Commission on Pacification's report of January 1991, during 1990 there were 3,346 politically motivated killings... By May 1991, about two thirds of the country was under state of emergency..." See: https://www.amnesty.org/fr/wp-content/uploads/2021/06/amr460361991en.pdf

The U.S. government has a very strict vetting process[4] for immigrants wishing to apply for visas. Applicants must have a criminal background check and a medical examination (e.g., immunization records, chest X-rays) provided by physicians accredited by the U.S. Embassy (with the results provided in a sealed envelope), in addition to other documents such as birth certificates, all of which needed to be obtained shortly before one's appointment. The process is both tedious and expensive, given all the processing fees incurred along the way. I'm not sure if the average American is aware of the many steps involved in becoming a U.S. citizen, or the many procedures that immigrants must follow before they can receive a visa.

Early in the morning of the fifth day, with my stack of documents in hand, Kathy and I had to find a way to get to the Embassy safely. Knowing about Lima's many fake "taxi drivers" (i.e., criminals who assaulted their passengers and dumped them in the streets), I told Kathy, "Let's choose a taxi driver who looks old." I figured there was less of a chance that we would be robbed by an old guy.

A steady stream of buses, trucks, and cars drove by us on the street as we stood near a noisy, exhaust-filled intersection. Finally, I spotted a Volkswagen "punch bug" with a gray-haired driver. I whistled hard and signaled for him to come our way. The driver saw me, made a U-turn, and stopped in front of us. As is customary in Peru, I asked the

---

[4] The U.S. immigration vetting process evolved from basic health checks at Ellis and Angel Islands to a rigorous, security-focused system. Today, it includes visa applications at consulates, background checks, biometric data collection, interviews, and medical exams, with heightened post-9/11 security measures.

driver how much he would charge to take us to the U.S. Embassy before we got into the car. He said it would cost $55 soles (about $13.75 U.S. dollars). It seemed a bit high to me, but maybe the driver thought Kathy was a rich American tourist—a common belief in developing countries. Nevertheless, I decided not to try to negotiate so we wouldn't have to spend too much time on the street. I quickly said, "Ok, let's go."

The driver got out of the car and walked around to open the passenger side door for us. At first, Kathy and I thought that it was nice of him to treat us like royalty. Then, we realized that the door handle and lock did not work. The driver had to undo the wire that was holding the door closed. We looked at each other, smiled, and got into the back seat of the old but cute taxi. The driver wired the door shut from the outside. Then, he ran around to his side of the car and started the car engine, which sounded like a diesel pickup truck. The inside of the taxi looked as if it had barely survived WWII. No upholstery was left on the doors, ceiling, or dashboard; it was all just metal. The accelerator pedal had a spring connected to the bottom of the steering wheel. The "car radio" was a battery-operated handheld device, which the driver had cleverly placed in the space where the original radio used to be. It was raining and luckily, the windows were closed. I didn't trust the handle to roll the windows down or up because it looked like it would fall off if we touched it. I expected the driver to turn on the windshield wipers to clear the water away so he could see. Instead, the driver pulled a handheld windshield wiper out from under his seat. He then stretched his left hand out the window and manually cleaned the windshield from the outside every 30 seconds or so while continuing to drive and simultaneously, giving us an update on the day's news. Kathy and I looked at each other and had to bite our lips to keep from laughing—we had never seen anything like it! The punch bug zigged and zagged between the lanes as the driver skillfully maneuvered through Lima's heavy traffic. We zipped through many red lights, and once or twice, came within centimeters of hitting other cars. If I needed proof that I was indeed back in Lima, that ride fit the bill!

After the hour-long ride, we finally reached the U.S. Embassy, alighted from the taxi, and paid the driver while expressing our gratitude. At the Embassy, we showed the security staff our passports and other forms of identification along with the letter proving that I had an appointment that day. After walking through the metal detector and running our bags through the x-ray machine, we made our way to the second floor.

My jaw almost hit the floor when we entered the waiting room. Not 10 feet in front of us, there was Mr. Rigby-Smith, the immigration officer who had rejected my tourist visa almost five years earlier! Naturally, a thousand thoughts rushed into my head, and I immediately broke out into a cold sweat even though things were different this time. We made eye contact from a distance, but thankfully, he didn't seem to recognize me. Once my name was called, the Embassy officials reviewed my INS documentation and separated Kathy and I into two different rooms

"Where do you work? When did you meet Kathy? Why did you marry her?" A flurry of cold, emotionless questions flew at me, one after the other. I felt as if I were in a cold-blooded interrogation room in a police station, guilty until proven innocent. "How often do you two go out? Where does she work? What color is her underwear? How long do you plan to live together?" The interview was humiliating. No human being should have to go through a process like this, where people representing a government agency trash the personal dignity of both you and your spouse. Over the years, I had been put down by people who thought they were superior to me often enough to recognize that the people interviewing us that day were members of the same not-so-distinguished club.

After about 20 minutes of answering the interrogator's— I mean, interviewer's—nitpicky and often intimate questions, Kathy was brought in from the other room. It was clear from the disgusted look on her face that she, too, had endured a similar "interview." I figured that now; my interviewer was going to continue torture session with her sitting next to me. Just then, a brilliant idea occurred to me. Just when the interrogator was about to resume his shaming rampage, I interrupted and said, "Excuse me, sir. We are in Lima, Peru, and in Peru, the official language is Spanish. So, I would like to continue this interview in Spanish, please."

Caught off guard at the unexpected interruption, the Embassy official seemed shocked by my request. He felt compelled to politely say, "uh… sure, let's switch to Spanish." As if someone had flipped a switch, his arrogance, misuse of authority and power, and superior attitude suddenly disappeared like air from a popped balloon. A short moment of silence invaded the room as he looked down at his list of questions. He started mumbling as he clumsily tried to put the next question together in Spanish. The phonetics of each word were completely off, and he had to repeat each word two or three times to make himself understood. He was sweating as he finally completed his first question. Despite myself, I couldn't help feeling a little bad for the guy. *How in the world did he get this job?* I thought to myself. As he finished asking his first question in Spanish, I could read in his expression that he was fervently hoping I had understood what he was saying. This time, he was the one who felt humiliated. The three of us knew the interview was over, but still, he was the only one with the power to end it. So, we played his game for a few more minutes until he finally said, in English, "I have no further questions. Come back at 2:00 pm to pick up your visa. Congratulations!"

I took Kathy for a walk to the park in Miraflores district, and we sat on the same bench where I had collapsed almost five years before after receiving the visa rejection. This time, I was on Cloud Nine. Facing the Pacific Ocean, holding hands with Kathy, listening to the birds singing and the gentle crashing of the waves, the expression, 'Heaven on Earth,' felt absolutely real and 100 percent attainable. We sat there for a long time, enjoying the sun's rays as they reflected off the ocean and dreaming about our future together.

After picking up the visa from the Embassy, we left Lima as quickly as possible, catching a flight to Arequipa the very next day. Coming back home for the first time by airplane was surreal. Five years had passed since I had left home to chase my American Dream. Looking at the magnificent volcanoes from the sky as the airplane descended brought tears to my eyes. *What a difference,* my heart whispered. My initial landing at Ronald Reagan National Airport in winter of 1987 was filled with intense, petrifying fear, but now, all I felt was peace.

"Flight attendants prepare for landing." The most beautiful words I have heard in my entire life. Who and how people welcome you determine how developed a society really is. The captain's bilingual message sparked a kind of euphoria and joy that is impossible to describe with mere words. As the airplane's tires touched the ground, I applauded with a shout of elation, inspiring the other passengers to also applaud and filling the AeroPerú jet with excitement. I felt like hugging all the passengers around me.

Mom, I am back. I'm back! I repeated silently as Kathy and I found our luggage and walked toward the terminal where the entire family awaited us. My family and I shed tears of joy as we reunited after almost half a decade apart, celebrating my long-awaited homecoming. Kathy finally met my parents and younger siblings. Like me, they all fell in love with my angel. They were surprised to hear Kathy speak Spanish so well.

After we all squeezed into my dad's 1960s Chevy[5] taxi, with my very excited youngest siblings sitting on our laps, we stopped to visit a few of my close relatives before returning to my childhood home. On the other side of my euphoric return was a harsh reality that I hadn't fully expected—my relatives were poorer and in even worse economic shape than they'd been five years earlier. I noticed that some seemed to think I was somehow "privileged" now, which

---

[5] In Peru, as in many countries in the developing world, most old American cars, whether from the 1960s or 1980s, are still used as regular vehicles. Working-class people often extend the lives of their vehicles by replacing parts or even adding modern engines and transmission systems from more affordable Asian car makers. It's cheaper for most people to keep their cars running longer instead of buying new ones. Some wealthy families save and preserve these classic American cars as antiques.

felt odd and made me uncomfortable. A few asked, "how much was the airplane ticket?" The answer made them to raise their eyebrows because the price of the tickets was unattainable from their vantagepoint, and without context, it seemed like a huge sum. I made a mental note to avoid talking about money whenever possible so no one would have to endure the awkward silence that such conversations inevitably brought.

We spent the next 10 days visiting my friends and extended family. Reuniting with my family and community was both pleasant and humbling. Some of cousins and my close friends were still unemployed. A few had been lucky enough to pass the college entrance exams and were studying in the local college. Others had left town to find work. I couldn't help but notice the interesting reactions from my friends and acquaintances when they realized that Kathy and I were married. While sitting with a group of my friends by the dusty soccer fields where we used to play as children, one of them said, "*te casaste con una gringa, wow, ahora vas a mejorar la raza.*" ("you married a gringa, wow, now you're going to improve our race!"). We all laughed, of course, but I knew that underneath all the jokes, they believed it was the truth.

Our visit flew by at lightning speed, and before we knew it, we found ourselves squeezing into the Chevy with my whole family, once again, to retrace our path back to the airport for our return to the U.S. We still cried as we said our goodbyes because we knew it would probably be at least a year before we would see each other again. But this time, we managed to mix a few laughs and smiles in with the tears because we knew it was just 'goodbye for now' and not 'goodbye forever.'

After returning to the U.S., Kathy and I slowly started stepping further into our world together, creating a new bi-cultural experience at the intersection of the United States and Peru that blended our different backgrounds, cultures, and traditions. Sometimes, we would go salsa dancing, make a delicious *Lomo Saltado,*[6] or treat ourselves to bowling or a movie and dinner at an all-you-can-eat buffet. Other times, we would just stay home. Kathy enjoyed reading, and I liked to draw or play my musical instruments.

The interactions between our worlds, which began with just the two of us, soon expanded to involve our family in the U.S. Kathy's sister was studying at a university not two hours from us, and she would occasionally visit us or vice versa. Dancing was a must whenever she came to town! In 1992, Kathy and I traveled to the Midwest for a family reunion, and that's where I met many of my new American relatives for the first time. I was surprised to learn that some of Kathy's great aunts still spoke German, even though they were second or third generation immigrants. Her Scottish and Polish family in Pennsylvania was smaller in number but just as caring and inclusive as the family in the Midwest. Kathy's paternal grandfather had migrated to America as a teenager before the Great Depression of the 1930s. Alt-hough I never got to meet him (he had died when Kathy was

---

[6] *Lomo Saltado* is a popular Peruvian dish that blends stir-fried beef with onions, tomatoes, and peppers and is typically served with French-fried potatoes and rice. This fusion of traditional Peruvian ingredients and seasonings with Asian stir-fry techniques reflects Peru's rich culinary diversity, influenced by Chinese immigration. Its vibrant flavors and hearty combination highlight Peru's innovative approach to blending cultures, making *Lomo Saltado* a standout in global cuisine and a symbol of Peru's culinary creativity.

10 years old), it felt good to know that he was a first-generation immigrant, just like me. Her paternal grandmother was also the daughter of a first-generation Polish immigrant. It was fascinating to connect with her family of fellow initiators of the American journey. Our worlds had indeed united in America.

Our "united state" became apparent in other dimensions of our lives, as well. Kathy greatly improved her Spanish, and my English improved, too, even though we adopted our own version of Spanglish at home. We would borrow words from one language when we couldn't find the correct word to express what we wanted to say in the other language. For example, I often told Kathy she was my *muñequita*. In Spanish, the word *muñequita* has a rich meaning that goes way beyond the standard English dictionary translation, "doll." It means cute, beautiful, gorgeous, young, and innocent, all at once.

Literal translations also became part of our homemade Spanglish. One night, I wanted to make sure that I didn't forget to call my Aunt Juana the next day to tell her about some important news from my dad. Just to be on the safe side, I asked Kathy to "remember me to Aunt Juana tomorrow." "What, did you die and forget to tell her?" Kathy quipped. That was when I learned that "remember me" and "remind me" mean two very different things, especially when you accidentally forget to say "call"! But I wasn't the only one prone to translation missteps. One night when we lost power in the apartment during a thunderstorm, Kathy exclaimed, "*¡Se fue el poder!*" She was trying to say, "We lost power!" But you can't translate that expression literally into Spanish. To me, it sounded like she was talking about some superhero who had suddenly lost his ability to fly in mid-air! Even though I knew what she meant, I couldn't help but burst out laughing. Over time, we corrected our flawed translations, but we kept using our best or cutest Spanglish expressions at home. Our bicultural experiences helped us to bond and grow, providing interesting perspectives and richness to our relationship.

Holy Resentments

As the honeymoon stage of our marriage faded, the love and chemistry that had initially brought us together were challenged by difficult clashes as we began to discover how different we were. Kathy was an independent, white, middle class, third-generation American citizen who had been raised in a liberal Lutheran home. I, on the other hand, was a conservative, brown, first-generation, Catholic immigrant, with a very different socio-cultural and linguistic upbringing. Interestingly, out of all our many cultural differences that could have caused problems, it was the religious beliefs assigned to us at birth that were the primary source of most of our arguments, resentments, and power struggles. Sometimes, it felt as if we were stuck in the early 1500s, still fighting about the protestant reformation!

Our fights weren't only about ideology; they were also fed by some of the same issues that come up in immigration debates, relating to differences between North American vs. South American and Latino vs. Euro-American values and lifestyles. There's a big difference between defending your perspective in a debate and actually living it in real time in your personal lives, of course, and our ability to try to understand each other's viewpoints and find solutions that worked for both of us was really being put to the test.

I was not only a Catholic, I was also a *South American* Catholic, which is very different from a *North American* Catholic. The South American Roman Catholic Church is deeply communal, and in Peru, religion is deeply intertwined with family life and public celebrations. It is deeply influential in Peru's cultural and societal norms, emphasizing social justice while blending Catholicism with indigenous traditions, a practice known as syncretism. Consequently, Peruvian Catholicism has unique practices that influence many aspects of daily life beyond just religion, such as education, politics, and the social hierarchy. In contrast, the North American Roman Catholic Church tends to place great emphasis on individual spirituality. Although faith practices may affect personal beliefs and choices, the Church's influence is less prominent outside the strict sphere of religion, probably due to North Americans' strong secular cultural values around individual rights and freedoms.

Although Kathy was brought up as a Lutheran, not a Catholic, some of her cousins were Catholic. From them, she had learned enough about American Catholic traditions to judge my "brand" of Catholicism as way, way too intrusive and conservative. I, on the other hand, was never exposed to protestant religions in Peru because they were virtually non-existent. Lutheranism was too new and liberal for me. Not only did I not understand it, I also had a need to defend "my church" tooth and nail because it felt like my core identity depended on it.

"My religion is the *true* religion," the Catholic within me often insisted, pissing off my (former!) angel Kathy. With her Lutheran upbringing, Kathy would come back at me with, "the Catholic church became so corrupt, it needed to be purged! Martin Luther did the right thing!" In our own private version of the religious battles that sparked the protestant reformation, we found many avenues for trying to advance our own religious agendas. Each of us staunchly defended our conservative or liberal perspectives on topics ranging from gay marriage and gun safety to reproductive health and race relations. These arguments triggered strong emotions, and we both refused to compromise our beliefs. I grew up convinced that Catholicism was the only true religion; all others were lost and needed to be "saved," from my perspective. Whenever Kathy was critical of my religion, it triggered me. I defended the Catholic tradition and what the church stood for, even if I, myself, did not fully agree with some of those beliefs. Religion became the source of constant power struggles between us, as we each sought to be the winner (or at least not the loser). Because we had plans to have children one day, we needed to reach a compromise. But religion was beginning to seem like a non-negotiable. Our crusade for righteousness was chipping away at the love between us and greatly damaging our marriage.

Once we finally realized that our constant arguments about religion were poisoning our relationship, we reached a compromised. Together, both of us would go to "my" church one Sunday and "her" church the following one. Although it seemed like a good idea at the time, this only made things worse. After the Lutheran services, I couldn't help but judge everything I disliked about the service and voice my observations aloud. "How can a female pastor be allowed to lead the service?" "Mother Mary was not even mentioned during the sermon today…" "Once again, I was the only person of color!" "The church looks and sounds so European." Having become aware of the importance of Native American teachings through my interactions with Chief Neale and my own spiritual journey, I noticed the lack of diversity among organized Euro-American religions. "We are on Native American land, and yet there's no mention at all about their teachings in the service," I added. Kathy, on the other hand, had her own list of unacceptable Catholic traditions. "How could an unmarried male priest talk about what is good for couples or women when he clearly has no clue what he's talking about?" "If God loved everyone, how could He punish people for being gay, lesbian, or queer?" Our Sunday battles continued to intensify, only adding to our lists of resentment against each other. I never thought religion would become a force with the power to potentially cripple or break up a family relationship.

"Did you marry me just for the papers?!" Kathy asked me accusingly one Sunday during yet another argument. I hadn't, of course, but the truth was that I *had* thought about ending our marriage many times during the difficult arguments about whose religion was better. I wondered if God would send me to straight hell if I claimed my freedom. But at the same time, I really did love Kathy, and the last thing I wanted to do was end our marriage. Even though I desperately wanted Kathy to agree to convert to Catholicism, I couldn't stomach the thought of trying to force or manipulate her into doing so by threatening to divorce her or go back to Peru. After a ton of inner debate, reflection, and prayer, I finally realized that to make what I felt was the right decision, I would have to go against the manmade interpretation of God and His laws.

Kathy must have come to a similar conclusion in her own reflections because sometime after our fourth year together, she and I finally managed to stop the madness that was damaging our relationship. "We're hurting ourselves too much over religion," Kathy said one day. "God must be crying to see His children fighting over which religion is better," I responded. We looked at each other, held hands, and decided to cut ties with organized religion and let love be our guide. The decision felt right, even sacred, and it allowed us to expand our inner sources of wisdom. It also gave us permission to learn from other sacred scriptures. We both still retained our Christian teachings, of course. But we also began to learn from the wisdom of other traditions, including ancient American cultures, which we now realized were also given to us by God, the Divine Creator.

Our past experiences had taught us to avoid "exclusionist" communities or ideologies. Instead, we sought out new, inclusive communities, congregations, and educational institutions. We also rediscovered new ways to enjoy each other's company, such as walks in nature, taking dance lessons, reading the newspaper together, and supporting each other in continuing our college educations. Slowly, our long lists of resentments began to fade. Detaching ourselves from organized religion was a paramount decision that brought quality to our lives. Ironically, in this process, we both also developed a greater appreciation for Mother Mary and Jesus as healers and teachers.

Invisible Scars, Unseen Justice

Little by little, the economy improved and with it, our job security improved a little, too. Kathy still worked for the temp agency, but the organization where she worked was using her services week after week, and she was beginning to feel like any other staff member at her office. I joined a union of restaurant and hospitality industry employees and had steady work at various hotels in the area—sometimes too much! The number of catering functions I was asked to cover increased significantly as the economy picked up. At the same time, I was studying at George Mason University and had a heavy course load. As the 1996 spring semester came to an end, and I was averaging only a few hours of sleep per night because I needed to finish my course work and prepare for final exams. The wear and tear of working so hard and studying so intensely was taking a big toll on me.

One evening during this crazy busy time, seventy or so banquet waiters and I were scheduled to serve at a prestigious dinner-dance function that a thousand people were expected to attend. Like the rest of the banquet staff, made up of first-generation immigrants, blacks, and a few whites,[7] I was setting up the tables in the ballroom area. Everyone was busy walking in and out of the ballroom, carrying plates, glasses, and silverware. Above the usual noise of screeching plates and utensils, someone suddenly screamed!

---

[7] In the late 1980s, the population of Washington, D.C. was 65-70% African American. The white population was declining due to suburban migration, while the Latino population was growing, largely due to civil unrest in Central America, particularly El Salvador.

A bunch of us ran into the ballroom to see what had happened. It turned out that one of the banquet captains, a Middle Eastern man known for his superiority complex, had slapped a middle-aged Bolivian waitress because she hadn't folded the napkins to his liking. I was outraged! I had never seen anything like it—not in Peru, and certainly not here.

My colleagues obviously felt the same way. Together, we confronted the captain, but he refused to apologize or show remorse. Instead, he continued to berate the waitress for her supposed sloppiness and all of us for coming to her aid. "She deserved it. Now get back to work!" he ordered. Within minutes, all 70 workers stopped what we were doing to stand in solidarity with our assaulted co-worker, who was still crying. "We are not going to let you treat us like this!" we yelled back. We continued arguing with the banquet captain for at least 20 minutes, and because the standoff showed no sign of abating, a few other banquet captains and hotel managers showed up to support the adamant and unyielding captain. "We have to open the doors to the guests in 5 minutes! Everyone calm down!" the head captain said, clearly on the verge of panic. "We will deal with this later, calm down!" The more they tried to pacify us, the more infuriated we became. In desperation, one of the managers called hotel security. They were obviously willing to do whatever it took to get us to go back to work. Finally, the head captain gave us an ultimatum, "If you don't stop this right now, we will fire every single one of you!"

Sadly, his words had their intended effect. Most of the banquet crew were recent immigrants and still in survival mode, and some were undocumented and simply couldn't afford to lose their jobs. Many had to support their undocumented family members or to send money home to children and spouses in their home countries. They couldn't risk fighting for their rights or being labeled as troublemakers. So, many of them—even those with documents—couldn't afford to report the abuse and injustice for fear of jeopardizing their jobs, or even their legal status. The hotel manager knew that, of course, and was banking on it. Confronted with the obvious imbalance in power and privilege, most of the workers stopped shouting the instant the head captain threw down his ultimatum. Some looked confused, others murmured among themselves. After a few seconds, most turned around and went back into the ballroom to finish setting up the tables even though they knew that the incident would never be reported.

I had had enough, however. My conscience wouldn't allow me to just pretend that the whole thing didn't happen. A feeling of disgust rose in my belly as I observed the whole psychological dynamic playing out in front of me. I wanted to be on the side that was just, the side that honored and respected all people, regardless of status. Along with about 10 other servers, I turned around and walked out. Just before leaving, I saw that one of the captains had opened the main doors, and the crew was greeting the guests with forced smiles, acting as if nothing had happened. I wondered if any of the guests would ever find out the true cost of their dinner that night, and if they did, whether they would care.

After the other 10 waiters and I walked out, five of us went to the apartment of another server to talk about what we had just experienced. We stayed for a couple of hours, and it was almost 2 am when everyone went home. Between all the emotional turmoil and having gotten up so early to study for finals, I was exhausted. Nevertheless, I gave one of the servers a ride home. About 10 minutes after dropping him off, my eyes began to close, despite the loud music I'd put on to keep myself awake. I rolled down the windows, hoping the fresh air would wake me up. But it was raining, so I quickly rolled the windows back up. Instead, I increased the volume of the radio even more. But within a few minutes, my eyes drifted closed again, and I fell sleep on the steering wheel while cruising along at 55 mph.

In Sickness and in Health

BAAAMMMMM!!!! A sound louder than thunder woke me up. I opened my eyes and for a second, everything was shaking violently, as if some external force was shaking the world. Then, I realized that the car was upside down and I was wedged against the steering wheel. The windshield was smashed, and rain was pouring on my face and soaking the inside of the car. The roof of the car was pressing hard against my head, and my legs were stuck in a bent position near the pedals.

"Help!! Help!!" I screamed over and over, but no one was around at 3 am on that rainy May morning. I tried using my legs to push myself out of the car, but no matter how hard I tried, nothing happened. I felt no pain at that moment, but my legs seemed to completely ignore the commands from my brain. In fact, I couldn't move a single muscle below my waist. I was scared, powerless, vulnerable, alone, and soaking wet. I did the only thing I could do. I turned to the Creator and prayed, *please send someone to rescue me when you have a chance.* Numbed by the temporary rush of endorphins and the exhaustion of a long day, I got a sense that everything was going to be ok, so I closed my eyes and fell sleep.

Maybe 30 minutes later, I felt someone tapping on my neck, "Hey, buddy, are you ok?" I woke up and saw a firefighter crouching down next to me. I heard fire engines and ambulances and saw flashing lights everywhere, half-blinding me. "I'm ok," I responded, but my voice sounded weak even to my own ears. Probably because my chest was pressed tightly against the steering wheel and the ceiling had twisted my neck to the side. "I am ok," I said again, and I answered to all the first responder's questions as he did a quick cognition check. "We're going to get you out of the car, buddy. Just close your eyes and stay still!" the first responder said above all the noise.

Next thing I knew, an electric saw was cutting a hole in the driver-side door and sparks were flying near my face. The rescue team laid me down carefully on a flat wooden stretcher and put a brace around my neck to prevent any further damage to my neck and back. Once they had gotten me into the ambulance, the paramedics rushed me to the local hospital in Manassas, Virginia. During the drive, one of the paramedics said that my car had driven off the road and hit a brick wall that supported a hard metal signpost in front of a small strip mall. The front tire had exploded with the force of the impact, which had probably lifted the car and turned it upside down before it landed in the empty parking.

As we drove, my natural reserve of endorphins began to run out, and by the time I arrived in the emergency room, the pain was unbearable. The emergency room staff kept me under observation for a few hours before ordering X-rays and MRI scans. Because the staff didn't yet know the full extent of my injuries, I was not allowed to drink, eat, or take any medicine. I screamed and cried for hours. The pain was excruciating! I was extremely thirsty and I felt like I was dying. The nurses who were monitoring me checked on me often. Every time a nurse came in the room, I begged for water and pain medicine. But they kept saying they couldn't give me anything yet. It was only after the MRI that the hospital staff finally gave me the pain medication that allowed me to fall sleep.

Whatever the X-rays and MRI revealed must have been bad because the next thing I remember was a wooshing sound. Strong gusts of swirling air enveloped me as the helicopter lifted off the ground with me in it! Weirdly, a flashback of the chopper at the U.S. border eight years earlier came to mind, and I desperately wanted to run and escape. I thought of Rosita and Pedro and everyone else in my "journey family" at the border, all trying to run to the bushes. But of course, hiding was impossible. With an oxygen mask covering my face, a brace on my neck, intravenous fluid lines in my veins, and my body strapped to a stretcher, I surrendered. Closing my eyes, I let the painkillers lull me to sleep again so I could travel to that unconsciousness place of dreams, where there is no pain.

I woke up in the recovery room at Fairfax Hospital. The staff had called Kathy while I was asleep to tell her what had happened, and of course, she had rushed to the hospital. The doctors told us that several vertebrae had been broken in my upper back. Two ribs were also broken, and my left ankle had been smashed. The worst part was that my back and spinal cord were severely damaged, and even with corrective surgery, there was a 99% chance that I would be paralyzed from the chest down for the rest of my life. Even though my head was foggy from the strong pain medicine I had been given, the news was so shocking that to this day, I still remember that conversation.

My angel Kathy signed the consent form that laid out all the risks and protected the doctors and hospital against any liability. Then, despite all the broken glass that was still embedded in my face, she kissed my bandaged forehead with tears in her eyes. That's the last thing I remember until I awoke many hours later. The surgery had lasted more than 9 hours, the nurse told me. It was an all-in-one surgery, where different specialized doctors had worked on different areas of the body at the same time. Once I was moved from the post-surgical area to the Intensive Care Unit (ICU), we called Peru to let my parents know that I had been hospitalized. I did my best to downplay the reason for my hospitalization, but my mother didn't buy it. She knew something very bad had happened, and she demanded to know the real story. So, I ended up telling her the truth. She wanted desperately to come take care of me, but she and my dad were on a long, 3-year waitlist for immigrant visas. Of course, Kathy was a U.S. citizen, and she promised my mom that she would request an emergency visa from the INS for her based on my medical situation. We all knew, however, that even that would take time and a lot of effort and luck.

For several weeks after the surgery, the doctors came to my bedside day after day to stick needles in my toes, hoping that I would feel a prick of pain. If I did, it would mean that my brain was receiving messages from the nerves in my lower body, which would prove that my spinal cord was doing its job and relaying those messages. But day after day, I felt nothing. Until finally one morning, the needle stick triggered a reflex and one of my big toes jerked a tiny bit. I think the doctor was as excited and exuberant as we were—it was a true miracle! It meant that I would not be completely paralyzed after all, and I would probably recover at least some motor skills in my lower extremities. We couldn't help but wonder if Kathy's grandmother Olive, who, in a crazy sequence of events, had passed away in Wisconsin literally minutes before my accident, was somehow protecting me and helping me recover. She and I had gotten along very well, and over the years, I'd grown to love her. In life, she had been the personification of love, but was it possible that she somehow became my guardian angel the instant she passed?

I certainly needed her help. Over the next few weeks, I worked harder than I'd ever worked in my life, just trying to regain a few basic motor skills. By this time, Fairfax Hospital had transferred me to an inpatient physical rehabilitation facility in Alexandria, Virginia. Life at that facility was a never-ending series of visits by pharmacologists, nurses, and various therapists—physical, occupational, respiratory, and speech language. After a lot of work, sweat, and intense pain (despite the pain meds), I was promoted to a wheelchair. That lead to weeks of even more work and pain as I learned to sit for longer and longer periods of time. At first, I could barely manage a few minutes. After about a month, I was up to about an hour, and I'd also learned to transfer myself from the bed to the wheelchair with the help of a walker by using my arms to pull myself up and support my bodyweight while Kathy maneuvered the wheelchair into position.

While I was grunting, sweating, and using all my will-power to strengthen my muscles and relearn skills as basic as sitting upright, Kathy was working hard to manage the deluge of paperwork that comes with being severely injured in a car wreck at the end of the school semester—auto insurance claims, health insurance claims, police reports, medical bills, doctor's appointments, university paperwork, the list went on and on—all while continuing to work full-time hours at her job. She also kept our promise to request an emergency visa from the INS for my mom so that once the doctor released me to come home, my mom could come to the U.S. to care for me during the day while Kathy was at work. Given that I was still completely unable to walk or otherwise use my paralyzed legs and lower body, it seemed like a reasonable request.

Hoping to further expedite the INS' review process, Kathy used her privilege as an educated U.S. citizen and resident of Virginia to enlist the support of a staffer who worked for our local congressman to put pressure on the U.S. Embassy in Lima to consider our emergency visa request sooner rather than later. About a week after Kathy submitted our request, the staffer faxed the Embassy a letter, signed by the congressman himself, inquiring about the status of our request. She might as well have waved a magic wand; not 24 hours after the Embassy received the fax, we got the wonderful news from the congressional staffer that our request had been approved, and that my mom should report to U.S. Embassy in Lima to pick up her emergency visa! My mom left for Lima the very next day, and she arrived in the U.S. right before the doctor discharged me from the hospital.

Soon after I managed to get myself from the bed to the wheelchair with minimal assistance from Kathy, despite my paralyzed legs, the doctor released me from the hospital to go home. Of course, I had to comply with certain conditions, like wearing a hard body brace, which stretched from my neck to my pelvis, at all times to protect my spine. I also had to keep doing physical, occupational, and respiratory therapy via home visits so I could continue building my strength, and, I hoped and prayed, eventually relearn how to use my legs, stand, and even walk.

Before I arrived home, my mom and Kathy carried our queen-sized bed from our bedroom on the second floor to the first-floor living room so I wouldn't have to climb the stairs, which would have been nearly impossible. Nevertheless, what used to be a short journey to the bathroom, just 10 steps away from the newly relocated bed, became a grueling half-hour ordeal. Since we didn't have a bathtub on the first floor, showers became a rare indulgence, requiring almost four laborious hours to get up the stairs, bathe, and come back down. With painstaking effort, my mom and Kathy would help lift me and the protective brace encasing my body as I sat on the floor and fought to pull myself up each step, inch by inch, using my upper body strength. Once I finally reached the shower, we had to carefully maneuver my body onto a plastic chair in the bathtub. The return trip left me drained and in pain, longing for the solace of sleep, which usually came immediately, once I'd finally collapsed onto the bed.

After a few months in the wheelchair while working relentlessly with my therapists to recover my strength and muscle function, my legs began to respond to the exercise and I graduated first, to standing, and then, to a walker. It was immensely gratifying to see how all the pain, sweat, and effort had paid off as I finally managed to take my first step. Kathy, my mom, and I celebrated with a special Peruvian dinner that my mom had made to mark my big achievement. In a few more days, one step became several, and my therapists told us I was on my way to regaining the ability to walk. *Thank you, Creator!*

As I continued improving and life slowly became a little less stressful, I was able to start joking and having fun again. My family and friends even started calling me 'the bionic man' because inside my body, I now had metal plates and screws everywhere. Six months ago, I couldn't have imagined ever being able to laugh about the accident; but now, laughter was just the medicine my soul needed to keep me moving forward.

Before I knew it, Thanksgiving arrived and for me, it was beyond meaningful. I was incredibly thankful to be alive and to Kathy, her family, and my mom. I was also grateful for the friends, relatives, acquaintances, and even strangers who had supported me. From the stranger who had seen me bleeding in the car and called for emergency response to all the people in the medical field—the paramedics, nurses, doctors, helicopter pilots, physical therapists, and cleaning crews. Despite my reservations and fears and the anti-immigrant sentiments that come and go every election cycle, I now understood that America is beautiful because of the caring human beings that inhabit it. The car accident had not just transformed my life, it also changed my perception of America and its people. I came to realize that I was living amongst angels, some of whom came from other countries and others who were born right here, and maybe where they came from mattered less than I'd thought.

Four months later, the numbness in my lower extremities had slowly been replaced by muscle strength, and I ditched the walker in favor of crutches. Life felt brand new as my mobility returned, and I began focusing on things outside myself once again, including school. It was around that time that something new and exciting began to capture my attention—the internet. When I first discovered the internet at school in the mid-'90s, it felt like crossing yet another border to a new universe. The dial-up tone was like a magical portal to a world where I could instantly access a vast library of knowledge. Each webpage that loaded and each chat with a stranger were exhilarating adventures into the unknown. Finding the internet was like finding a hidden treasure chest filled with endless possibilities and new connections.

After returning to my classes at George Mason University, the school's computer lab became my second home. I decided to teach myself how to build websites and create animations. Along the way, I learned several programming languages and mastered file transfers and other processes (many of which are totally automated today). By the time I was able to walk with the help of just a cane, I was ready to graduate from George Mason University with a bachelor's degree in marketing, augmented with the expertise I'd developed on my own in the new field of web development. This combination helped me to get my first job as a web designer. Over the next few years, I continued improving my skills on the job, which enabled me to advance quickly up the web design food chain and become first, a web developer and later, a software applications developer.

A Renewed Passion for Life in America

By 2008, I was working first as a full-time software applications developer at George Washington University's (GWU) Medical Center. Each May, I still took time to pause and reflect on the accident and how much it had changed both my life and my life trajectory. At GWU, my late friend and colleague, Paul Tschudi, GWU professor of grief counseling, showed up as my next angel. A caring and wise Vietnam veteran, Paul looked behind my software developer persona and noticed the counselor/healer/paqo who had been percolating deep within me for a long time. He was fundamental in my transition from the logical world of computers to the person-centered counseling profession. With Paul's encouragement and support, I immersed myself in the field of mental health counseling over the next decade, completing first, a master's degree and then, a doctoral degree at George Mason University in March of 2019, at age 50. After graduating, I became an adjunct professor in the counseling program and taught online and in-person courses at my alma mater during the Covid-19 pandemic, while working as a mental health counselor in domestic and sexual violence with the Fairfax County Government. As I gained experience in the counseling profession, I felt much more aligned than I had as a software applications developer. With time, I began to extend my work in counseling to also incorporate nature and indigenous knowledge systems.

Back in the early 2000s, Kathy and I had begun participating in spiritual and healing circles to fill the gap that had been created when we'd left organized religion. Before long, we transitioned from being participants to becoming facilitators in the spiritual arena. Feeling strongly called to nourish our physical, emotional, and spiritual sides in an integrated way, we began sharing and helping people learn from the teachings of ancient and modern cultures, including Native North and South American teachings. We began offering self-care workshops, which we held at our home, in local parks, or occasionally, at friends' homes. We also began leading groups on sacred journeys to Peru. What had started as mere participation in informal gatherings of like-minded people turned into powerful annual journeys that expanded peoples' understanding of life, themselves, and their relationships as they connected with the energy of the sacred Inkan sites.

Today, Kathy and I dedicate all our time to Eagle Condor Center (https://www.eaglecondorcenter.org), our private holistic practice in Northern Virginia, focusing in two main areas. At the *organizational level,* I offer consulting and training on immigrant integration and inclusion and cultural competence. These services are provided for behavioral healthcare, family service delivery, and non-profit organizations. Occasionally, we team up with non-profit organizations to provide free or low-cost nature-based retreats specifically for Spanish-speaking immigrants. We call these events *"Encuentro con lo Nuestro"* (connecting with our heritage) where participants explore and deepen their connection to their culture with the goal of increasing their sense of belonging, addressing feelings of grief and loss, and building resilience. At the *individual and family level,* we blend evidence-based and nature-based consulting and coaching, vibrational astrology, and indigenous healing systems for holistic healing and well-being. Our healing modalities include workshops, self-care retreats, and group journeys to Peru.

Home Is Anywhere There Is Love

In the Summer of 2006, Kathy and I took a family trip to visit my parents-in-law, now living in Arizona, along with our two sons, who had been born a few years earlier, and my sister-in-law and her two children. My father-in-law, a retired sales executive, had spent his career driving on just about every road in the continental U.S., and he was an expert at finding shortcuts. If there was a new road to travel, he knew exactly how to find it in the extensive collection of maps he kept in his car. (This was obviously before the GPS era.) After an amazing visit to the Grand Canyon, we needed to get back to Gerome, Arizona, a former ghost town known for its art and antique stores, which was about three hours away. After studying his maps carefully for several minutes, my father-in-law said, "According to my map, there is a shortcut we can take to Gerome to arrive in about two hours instead of the usual three." We agreed that sounded like a good plan. "We'll have to drive on a dirt road for about half an hour, though," he warned. We all nodded in agreement and said we would follow his lead.

After forty-five minutes of driving along the dirt road, we stopped in the middle of the desert, totally confused. The wind was blowing some dust gently in different directions, and tall cactus plants surrounded us on both sides of the road, seeming to stare at us, as if wondering, *what is the deal with these people*? Worried, my father-in-law and his daughters stared at the map, trying to figure out where we were and if we had taken a wrong turn. Meanwhile, I walked a few yards, looked out at the horizon, and suddenly felt an unexpected sense of peace in the silence of the dry, dusty, rocky geography that surrounded us. At first, my mind took me to the Western movies, but as I went deeper into the daydream state that had taken hold of me, I felt absorbed by the strong Apache presence in the air. It felt like an ancient, nurturing energy was lifting my spirit, and I noticed the similarities of the geography and ecosystem of the land to the outskirts of my native Arequipa. As I gazed around at the cacti, birds, dust, and dry grass, I was aware that under each rock, different types of life were hidden from view but still very present. I felt a shower of subtle energy vibrations flowing through me, from the top of my head to my feet, as if the ancient Mother wanted me to pay attention. I became a child, and as I allowed the energy to flow through me freely, I felt completely aligned with the Great Mother Earth. The 10-second experience provided me with a clear and timeless message: *You are one with nature. Whether you are in Arequipa or Arizona, you are home. Wherever you are, you are home.*

I don't think more than 10 minutes had passed since I had left the caravan; but as I walked back to my family, I felt as if I had just returned from a vision quest.[8] It was as if time

---

[8] A Native American vision quest is a sacred spiritual practice among tribes like the Lakota, Apache, and Ojibwe, serving as a rite of passage and a means of seeking spiritual guidance. It involves fasting, solitude, and meditation in nature, often for several days. The quest begins with a purification ceremony, such as a sweat lodge, to prepare the individual. During the quest, the person prays and remains open to receiving a vision from the spirit world. This vision provides profound personal insight and direction. Upon returning, the quester shares their experience with a spiritual leader for interpretation and integration.

had stopped, and an avalanche of teachings had been bestowed. I had felt the Apache spirits who dwelled on that land. They had revealed themselves to bring me this new awareness. The Apache wisdom, as I like to call this memorable moment, had shaken up all my preconceptions about my identity and given me a renewed perspective of life. Now, I knew that no matter how far I traveled, I was always at the center of the compass—the center of the four directions—always home. This realization was both an answer and a confirmation that brought a higher level of consciousness to my search for identity.

It took many years to fully believe that I was always home in the U.S., though. Feeling a true sense of belonging in America is one of the hardest things to achieve for most first-generation immigrants because of all the messages to the contrary that continually bombard us. When people tell us to "go back where you came from," or say, "if you report or complain, I will call immigration on you," it increases our fears and makes integration that much harder. How much fear we carry depends on many things—our experiences on our journeys, country of origin, legal status, level of formal instruction, and exposure to xenophobia, anti-immigrant sentiments, racism, violence, and the legal system. The more anti-immigrant narratives we are exposed to, the longer we feel foreign, unwelcome, and alienated.

What's so paradoxical is that the perception portrayed in these narratives—that new immigrants reject American culture and don't want to integrate—couldn't be further from reality! The truth is that most immigrants want nothing more than to integrate into their new culture as quickly as possible. I can't help but wonder, what if, instead of criticizing us for being different and not "American enough," long-time Americans put out their hands and helped us to become as American as they are? Acting in ways that promote integration at the individual level is how we all—both immigrants and long-time Americans—can contribute to national healing. Chief Joseph Raincrow Neale understood this, and his actions, when he treated me like a brother, validated my journey to America, helping me to feel like a human being who was genuinely welcome on this land.

Years after my experience in the Arizona desert, the wisdom imparted by the ancient Apache spirits was reinforced and grounded by the teachings of the Oglala Lakota Elder Black Elk,[9] who had this to say about our true home:

> The first peace, which is the most important, is that which comes within the souls of men when they realize their relationship, their oneness with the universe and all its Powers, and when they realize that at the center of the universe dwells Wakan Tanka, and that this center is everywhere, it is within each of us.

As Black Elk expressed so eloquently, the truth is that the soul knows no borders. When this is acknowledged, all that is left is a sense of belonging, a sense of home. It's essential to remember that we are all part of a bigger family—the

---

[9] In "Black Elk Speaks," John G. Neihardt recounts the life of Black Elk, an Oglala Sioux elder and holy man. Black Elk shares his profound visions and experiences, including his role as a spiritual leader during a time of great upheaval for his people. He witnessed the decimation of the Lakota way of life due to the encroachment of white settlers. Through his visions and ceremonies, Black Elk sought to preserve his culture and provide spiritual guidance. His story is a testament to resilience and spiritual depth.

human family. When we acknowledge that, we honor the universal truth that home is everywhere, and we all belong.

The "American Dream" led me to my home, America, but it took a life-long, journey of thousands of miles to understand that it doesn't matter where we live, our home is everywhere. Woody Guthrie put it beautifully when he sang... "This land is your land, this land is my land ...this land was made for you and me!" This understanding has inspired me in my later years to give back with gratitude by helping immigrants like Rosita and her son as well as people from all walks of life, regardless of race or nationality. And that is my living dream.

The Boy is Home

In the turbulence of his youth
The boy found a strand of hope
Born from images on a screen

The American Dream crawled into his dreams
His soul saw no borders, and off he went
Arriving unprepared for the winter blues

Survival occupied all waking thought
No job was too small or too low
Was the boy's dream just a beautiful lie?

Silent tears held his family together from afar
The alien boy mastered fear, embraced challenge
While *Nowhere Man* played in his heart

His flute gently searched for answers in the wind
His desire to belong met the Sun's smile from above
As the eagle and the condor glided through the sky

"Welcome, my brother!" The Indian said
"How can I help, amigo?" a White friend offered
"May we dance together?" the young woman asked

The healing has begun
Love unifies the world and has no borders
Nowhere Man is welcome at last

The dream has come true against the odds
The alien is gone, and the boy is home
Home, where he is welcomed and loved

~ Ricardo O. Sánchez

Photo 7. Receiving my doctorate in counseling and human development from GMU in 2019.

EPILOGUE

America the Beautiful

"Aho Mitákuye Oyás'iŋ" (We are all related.)

~ Lakota Proverb

Americans and immigrants alike are concerned about the polarization of ideas and narratives in today's United States, and almost everyone longs for a *re-United States of America* based on our highest principles. The beauty of America is within us, it is in focusing on what we share and what unites us. We share common values such as a desire for a better life, the American Dream, an entrepreneurial spirit, freedom, and equality. We share a passion for music and concerts, delicious fusion food, good movies and TV shows, and sports. We share stadiums to cheer on our favorite teams and players, whether we prefer Lionel Messi's soccer or LeBron James' basketball. We come together at concert halls to enjoy old favorites like Bruce Springsteen or contemporary singers like Taylor Swift or Shakira. We all appreciate nature's beauty, and we enjoy outdoor activities at parks, the beach, or in the mountains. We respect history and our ancestors, including Indigenous people, without whom many would not have survived to celebrate the first Thanksgiving. We share so many celebrations—Cinco de Mayo, Halloween, Día de los Muertos, Christmas, New Year's, and many, many more. We have been dancing together for ages. I have heard Americans ask, "what would life be like without tacos?" And I know for sure that the American Dream would be incomplete without a good smash burger from a food truck. The list of commonalities is endless. The fact is, we are one big family living side by side on an ancient and beautiful land. We have gone through so many things together, and it's in our best interest now to show our heartfelt appreciation and care for each other in our daily interactions.

Our souls come to this world to experience being human, and when our journey ends, we return to nature. As humans, we are citizens of Earth, beyond the labels of documents. Documents help maintain societal order, but when used to categorize, discriminate, or marginalize, they violate the essence of humanity and dehumanize our shared experience. Labeling people by legal status sets harmful processes into motion, creating divisions. Some feel entitled; others live in fear or shame. This culture of separation and xenophobia affects us all. I invite you to consider a better way.

I refuse to believe that our nation is divided beyond repair. Rather, it is profoundly distracted. This distraction has moved us away from our nation's core values and our individual principles. The focus has shifted to polar extremes, which are highly charged and pull everyone in different directions. Passionate pre- and post-election sentiments are driving a discourse filled with despair and fear for some and revenge for others—none of this will put us on the path to regaining our strength, finding central commonalities, and healing.

I am not suggesting neutrality or hiding our head in the sand. On the contrary, we all need to remain active and attuned with the force of alignment—alignment of your own core principles and the highest values of our nation. Speak up when the charged poles try to pull you into despair or vengeance. You are neither! Despair and vengeance are among the opposite of well-being. Instead, use love and compassion to bring yourself and all of us back into alignment. Doing this can be our best contribution as citizens of this great nation.

Ten Commandments for Humanity

My invitation is to shift our focus toward re-igniting the passions that bring us together and to foster unity among families and communities across America. What if we re-imaged all of us getting along? Coexisting while embracing and honoring our differences? I offer these suggestions as a sort of "ten commandments for humanity," to help heal divisiveness and return the United States to true greatness.

1. Welcome a migrant as you wish to be welcomed.
2. Be patient and compassionate with those new to your community; everyone needs time to adjust.
3. Recognize and honor their journeys and struggles; they left behind everything familiar to join your community.
4. Get to know your neighbors personally, not through stereotypes.
5. Make strangers feel at home by extending kindness.
6. Show love and respect to all, we are all members of the human family.
7. Value each person's identity, virtues, and aspirations, regardless of their background.
8. Practice true inclusion and unity to bridge divides.
9. Be a guiding light for those in need, remembering that every human life has inherent worth.
10. Stay true to your highest principles and uphold the core values that define our nation.

Photo 8. Sharing our work at Eagle Condor Center at a presentation in Virginia.

Photo 9. Machu Picchu during a group journey to Peru. The journey is a unique 10-day program that incorporates Andean knowledge systems and nature-based healing techniques that complement participants' own life journeys.

Glossary of Terms

Alliance for Progress: A U.S. initiative launched in 1961 by President John F. Kennedy aimed at fostering economic cooperation, development, and reform in Latin America to counter the influence of communism and improve relations between the United States and Latin American countries.

American Dream: The idea that every individual, regardless of their background or circumstances, has the opportunity to achieve success, prosperity, and upward social mobility through hard work, determination, and personal effort. Rooted in the values of freedom, equality, and opportunity, it suggests that with perseverance, anyone can attain a better life—often symbolized by owning a home, having a stable career, and securing a bright future for one's family.

"Brain Drain": This term refers to the emigration of highly skilled or educated individuals from one country to another. This phenomenon typically occurs when professionals, scientists, engineers, or other highly qualified individuals leave their home country in search of better career opportunities, higher salaries, or improved living conditions. The term highlights a situation where the departure of talented individuals can have negative effects on the home country, such as a loss of intellectual and technical expertise, which can hinder its economic development and innovation capabilities.

Central Intelligence Agency (CIA): A U.S. federal agency that played a significant role in Latin America during the Cold War. Responsible for coordinating government intelligence activities outside the U.S., the CIA conducted covert operations aimed at countering

Soviet influence and preventing the spread of communism in the region. Through activities such as intelligence gathering, political manipulation, and the orchestration of coups, it intervened in the internal affairs of several Latin American countries.

Department of Homeland Security (DHS): A U.S. federal agency created in 2003 in response to the September 11 attacks. It replaced the Immigration and Naturalization Service (INS), which was dissolved upon the creation of DHS. The INS' responsibilities were split among three new agencies within DHS: 1) U.S. Citizenship and Immigration Services (USCIS), which handles immigration benefits such as citizenship and green cards; 2) U.S. Immigration and Customs Enforcement (ICE), which enforces immigration law and handles deportations; and 3) U.S. Customs and Border Protection (CBP), which manages border security and immigration at ports of entry.

Dependency theory: Dependency theory asserts that U.S. influence over Latin American nations is rooted in a structural economic imbalance, where these nations are exploited for their resources while remaining economically dependent on more developed countries. This dynamic reinforces inequality and limits development, as Latin American economies are designed to benefit the U.S., perpetuating a cycle of underdevelopment.

Emigration: Emigration is the act of leaving one's home country to settle permanently in another. People emigrate for various reasons, such as better job prospects, education, political stability, or to escape conflict. Emigration refers to the departure from the origin country, as opposed to immigration, which refers to arrival in a new country.

Gringo/a: The word "gringo" likely originated from the Spanish word *griego* (Greek). It was initially used to describe something foreign or unintelligible, similar to the English phrase "It's all Greek to me." Different theories suggest it evolved from slang from Spain's Andalusian region, Portuguese influence, or the Mexican-American War, though these are less substantiated. The term was documented in Spain as early as the 18th century, referring to foreigners, particularly those who struggled with the Spanish language. Over time, it came to refer more specifically to white English-speaking foreigners in Latin America.

Immigration and Naturalization Service (INS): An agency of the U.S. Department of Justice from 1933 to 2003. It was responsible for enforcing immigration laws, managing immigration benefits, and overseeing the naturalization process in the United States. The INS handled the admission of immigrants, processed visa applications, managed deportation procedures, and coordinated matters related to asylum and refugees.

Migration: Human migration is the movement of people from one place to another, often across regions or countries, for various reasons such as seeking better opportunities, escaping conflict, or due to environmental changes. It can be voluntary or forced, and affects cultural, social, and economic dynamics globally.

Mestizo: Referring to a person of mixed ancestry, specifically a person descended from both European (typically Spanish) and Indigenous parents, it essentially means "mixed person" in Spanish. It is a term used across Latin America to describe individuals with a blended heritage from these two racial backgrounds.

Navigation Capital: Refers to the skills, knowledge, and resources that immigrants develop to effectively navigate and adapt to new social, cultural, and institutional systems in a host country. This concept includes understanding how to access essential services, education, healthcare, and employment, as well as navigating legal systems and overcoming language barriers. Navigation capital is crucial for immigrants to thrive in unfamiliar environments, helping them integrate while maintaining resilience in the face of challenges such as discrimination or systemic obstacles.

Non-Governmental Organizations (NGOs): Independent, non-profit entities that play a significant role in providing humanitarian assistance in Latin America. They typically focus on areas like health, education, and disaster relief. However, their involvement is sometimes controversial because some have been accused of serving the political agendas of external governments or local elites. These instances raise concerns about NGOs' role and soft power, undermining their legitimacy as neutral, humanitarian agencies.

Remote Acculturation: A modern process of cultural exchange that occurs when people are exposed to a distant culture through indirect or intermittent means. It's a type of globalization-facilitated acculturation via trade, technology, tourism, and transnationalism. Within the context of Latin American migration, remote acculturation evolved as a unidirectional influence, from industrialized to developing nations via radio, television, film and the entertainment industry. This influence occurred through the transmission of industrialized nations' narratives and cultural products, leading to the adoption of certain aspects of culture, including lifestyle, fashion, language, behavior, and values. The adopted elements blended with the developing nation's own traditions, sometimes at the expense of preserving its original cultural identity.

Bibliography

Aguilar, H. A. (2014). *"Los deportados": The transnational blowback of the United States deportation practices and the hidden costs of mass deportation* (Master Thesis). Retrieved from http://ebot.gmu.edu/handle/1920/8680

Asner-Self, K. K., & Marotta, S. A. (2005). Developmental indices among Central American immigrants exposed to war-related trauma: Clinical implications for counselors. *Journal of Counseling & Development*, 83(2), 162–171.

Ataiants, J., Cohen, C., Riley, A. H., Tellez Lieberman, J., Reidy, M. C., & Chilton, M. (2017). Unaccompanied children at the United States border, a human rights crisis that can be addressed with policy change. *Journal of Immigrant and Minority Health*. https://doi.org/10.1007/s10903-017-0577-5

Barnert, E., Stover, E., Ryan, G., & Chung, P. (2015). Long journey home: Family reunification experiences of the disappeared children of El Salvador. *Human Rights Quarterly*, 37(2), 492–510.

hooks, b. (2009). Belonging: A culture of place. Routledge.

Becerra, D. (2016). Anti-immigration policies and fear of deportation: A human rights issue. *Journal of Human Rights and Social Work*, 1(3), 109–119. https://doi.org/10.1007/s41134-016-0018-8

Benuto, L. T., Casas, J. B., Gonzalez, F. R., & Newlands, R. T. (2018). Being an undocumented child immigrant. *Children and Youth Services Review*, 89, 198–204. https://doi.org/10.1016/j.childyouth.2018.04.036

Bruneau, T. (2016). *The United States and Central America: From stopping communism to stopping kids*. Retrieved from http://calhoun.nps.edu/handle/10945/49184

Chomsky, A. (2014). *Undocumented: How immigration became illegal*. Boston, MA: Beacon Press.

Chomsky, N. (2017). *The crisis of immigration.* Retrieved from
https://www.youtube.com/watch?v=ttSxhONuPRM&in-
dex=2&list=PLLAkS9OasUapZW_xZbsAdcxstT-
7u0Nnw&t=24s

Clayton, C. (1999). *Peru and the United States: The condor and the eagle.*
University of Georgia Press.

Colburn, F. D., & Arturo, C. S. (2016). Trouble in the "northern triangle." *Journal of Democracy, 27*(2), 79–85.
https://doi.org/10.1353/jod.2016.0024

Dreby, J. (2012). The burden of deportation on children in Mexican
immigrant families. *Journal of Marriage and Family, 74*(4), 829–845.
https://doi.org/10.1111/j.1741-3737.2012.00989.x

Dreby, J. (2015). US immigration policy and family separation: The
consequences for children's well-being. *Social Science & Medicine,
132*, 245–251.

Durand, J. (2010). *The Peruvian diaspora* (M. Ortega Breña, Trans.).
ReVista: Harvard Review of Latin America, 9(2), 50-52.

Fejes, F. (1981). Imperialism, media, and the good neighbor: New
Deal foreign policy and United States shortwave broadcasting to
Latin America. *Journal of Communication, 31*(3), 90-103.

Ferguson, G., Tran, S., Mendez, S., & van de Vijver, F. (2017). Remote acculturation: Conceptualization, measurement, and implications for health outcomes. In S. J. Schwartz & J. Unger (Eds.),
The Oxford Handbook of acculturation and health (pp. 157–174). Oxford University Press. https://doi.org/10.1093/ox-
fordhb/9780190215217.001.0001

Gil-Garcia, O. G. (2018). US immigration enforcement and the
making of unintended returnees. *Human Development Faculty Scholarship,* 16.

Goizueta, R.S. (2004). The symbolic realism of U.S. Latino/a popular Catholicism. *Theological Studies, 65*(2), 255-274.

Gonzalez, L. R. (2016). *Guatemalan unaccompanied children migration: A
case study of unaccompanied children in Guatemala.* Retrieved from
https://repositories.lib.utexas.edu/handle/2152/39094

Goodman, A. (2017). The long history of self-deportation: Trump's
anti-immigrant policies build on more than a century of attempts to create fear and terror within U.S. immigrant communities. *NACLA Report on the Americas, 49*(2), 152–158.
https://doi.org/10.1080/10714839.2017.1331811

Goodman, R., Vesely, C. K., Letiecq, B., & Cleaveland, C. L. (2017). Trauma and resilience among refugee and undocumented immigrant women. *Journal of Counseling & Development, 95*(3), 309–321. https://doi.org/10.1002/jcad.12145

Gott, R. (2002, June 5). *Fernando Belaúnde.* https://www.theguardian.com/news/2002/jun/06/guardianobituaries2

Goździak, E. M. (2015). What kind of welcome? Integration of Central American unaccompanied children into local communities. *Institute for the Study of International Migration, 42.*

Hillou, D. (2017, March 5). *A climate of fear: The social impact of the Trump administration's immigration policies.* Retrieved May 4, 2018, from American University Journal of Gender, Social Policy & the Law website: http://www.jgspl.org/climate-fear-social-impact-trump-administrations-immigration-policies/

Hurtado-de-Mendoza, A., Serrano, A., Gonzales, F. A., Fernandez, N. C., Cabling, M. L., & Kaltman, S. (2016). Trauma-exposed Latina immigrants' networks: A social network analysis approach. *Journal of Latina/o Psychology, 4*(4), 232–247. https://doi.org/10.1037/lat0000053

Jonas, S. (2013, March 27). *Guatemalan migration in times of civil war and post-war challenges. Migration Policy Institute.* https://www.migrationpolicy.org/article/guatemalan-migration-times-civil-war-and-post-war-challenges

Keller, H. (2016). Attachment. A pancultural need but a cultural construct. *Current Opinion in Psychology, 8*, 59–63. https://doi.org/10.1016/j.copsyc.2015.10.002

Kellner, D. (2020). Liberty, equity, and U.S. foreign policy contradictions in Latin America. *Latin American Politics and Society, 63*(2), 123-141.

Krogstad, J. M. (2016, May 4). *U.S. border apprehensions of families and unaccompanied children jump dramatically.* Retrieved May 22, 2017, from Pew Research Center website: http://www.pewresearch.org/fact-tank/2016/05/04/u-s-border-apprehensions-of-families-and-unaccompanied-children-jump-dramatically/

Labrador, R. C., & Renwick, D. (2018, January 18). *Central America's violent northern triangle* [Council on Foreign Relations]. Retrieved May 14, 2018, from Council on Foreign Relations website: https://www.cfr.org/backgrounder/central-americas-violent-northern-triangle

Lopez, M. E. (2010). *My heart was over there with you and I was here: Exploring the immigration narratives of families separated during the course of migration.* Retrieved from https://escholarship.org/uc/item/8pq635k6.pdf

Magnelli, A., Maia, F., & Martins, P. H. (Eds.). (2024). *Dependency theories in Latin America.* Routledge.

Mattelart, A. (1979). *Multinational corporations and the control of culture: The ideological apparatuses of imperialism.* Harvester Press.

Meacham, J. (2018). *The soul of America: The battle for our better angels.* Random House.

Menjívar, C., Abrego, L. J., & Schmalzbauer, L. (2016). *Immigrant families.* Malden, MA: Polity Press.

Miville, M. L., & Ferguson, A. D. (2014). Intersections of race-ethnicity and gender on identity development and social roles. In M. L. Miville & A. D. Ferguson (Eds.), *Handbook of race-ethnicity and gender in psychology* (pp. 3–21). Retrieved from http://link.springer.com/10.1007/978-1-4614-8860-6

Neihardt, J. G. (1972). *Black Elk speaks: Being the life story of a holy man of the Oglala Sioux* (3rd ed.). New York, NY: Pocket.

Palacio, G. (2012). An eco-political vision for an environmental History: Toward Latin American and North American research partnership. *Environmental History, 17*(4), 725–743.

Penaloza, L. N. (1989). *Immigrant consumer acculturation.* ACR North American Advances, NA-16. Retrieved from http://acrwebsite.org/volumes/6890/volumes/v16/NA-16

Perreira, K. M., & Ornelas, I. (2013). Painful passages: Traumatic experiences and post-traumatic stress among U.S. immigrant Latino adolescents and their primary caregivers. *International Migration Review, 47*(4), 976–1005. https://doi.org/10.1111/imre.12050

Phipps, R. M., & Degges-White, S. (2014). A new look at transgenerational trauma transmission: Second-generation Latino immigrant youth. *Journal of Multicultural Counseling and Development, 42*(3), 174–187. https://doi.org/10.1002/j.2161-1912.2014.00053.x

Religion & Culture (2023, October 11). *Divergent Perspectives: The Unique Views of White and Hispanic Catholic Americans.* Retrieved October 7, 2024, from PRRI website :https://www.prri.org/spotlight/divergent-perspectives-the-unique-perspectives-of-white-and-hispanic-catholic-americans/#:~:text=Satisfaction%20with%20Church%20Leadership%20and,more%20women%20in%20Church%20leadership.

Rojas, S. M., Grzywacz, J. G., Zapata Roblyer, M. I., Crain, R., & Cervantes, R. C. (2016). Stressors among Hispanic adults from immigrant families in the United States: Familismo as a context for ambivalence. *Cultural Diversity and Ethnic Minority Psychology, 22*(3), 408.

Roman, E. (1998). The alien-citizen paradox and other consequences of U.S. colonialism. *Florida State University Law Review, 26*, 1-47.

Sánchez, R. O. (2019). *Immigrant family reunification among Central American undocumented minors in the U.S.: Implications for counseling.* (Doctoral Dissertation). Retrieved from https://pqdtopen.proquest.com/pubnum/13864554.html

Sánchez, R. O., Letiecq, B. L., & Ginsberg, M. R. (2019). An integrated model of family strengths and resilience: Theorizing at the intersection of indigenous and western paradigms. *Journal of Family Theory & Review, 11*(4), 561–575. https://doi.org/10.1111/jftr.12351

Sawyer, C. B., & Márquez, J. (2017). Senseless violence against Central American unaccompanied minors: Historical background and call for help. *The Journal of Psychology, 151*(1), 69–75. https://doi.org/10.1080/00223980.2016.1226743

Schiller, H. I. (2017). Communication and cultural domination. Routledge.

Schlesinger, S., & Kinzer, S. (2021). Ambiguous influence: U.S. foreign policy in Latin America. *World Politics Quarterly, 58*(1), 34-52.

Schoultz, L. (1987). *National security and United States policy toward Latin America.* Princeton University Press.

Schueths, A. M. (2012). Barriers to interracial marriage? Examining policy issues concerning U.S. citizens married to undocumented Latino/a immigrants. *Journal of Social Issues, 68*(1), 133-148. https://doi.org/10.1111/j.1540-4560.2011.01740.x

Suárez-Orozco, Carola. (2017). Conferring disadvantage: Behavioral and developmental implications for children growing up in the shadow of undocumented immigration status. *Journal of Developmental & Behavioral Pediatrics, 38*, 424–428.

Economic Policy Institute. (2021). *More than $3 billion in stolen wages recovered for workers between 2017 and 2020*. Retrieved from https://www.epi.org

Zentgraf, K. M., & Chinchilla, N. S. (2012). Transnational family separation: A framework for analysis. *Journal of Ethnic and Migration Studies, 38*(2), 345–366. https://doi.org/10.1080/1369183X.2011.646431

About the Author

Ricardo O. Sánchez is co-director of Eagle Condor Center, a private practice group in Virginia. He received his PhD in Counseling and Human Development in 2019 from George Mason University, where he teaches as an adjunct professor. He has worked with immigrant families on topics related to family reunification, unaccompanied minors, and domestic conflicts. He provides consulting and training on immigrant integration and inclusion, cultural competence, and promoting social inclusion and equity. In his practice, he blends evidence-based and nature-based consulting and indigenous healing systems for holistic healing and well-being.

For further information about Eagle Condor Center, visit the website:
www.eaglecondorcenter.org

www.ingramcontent.com/pod-product-compliance
Lightning Source LLC
Chambersburg PA
CBHW070031100426
42740CB00013B/2662